Annie Broadhead | Ginni Light

English for Personal Assistants

The essential handbook for
doing business internationally

GABLER

Bibliographic information published by Die Deutsche National Bibliothek
Die Deutsche National Bibliothek lists this publication in the
Deutsche Nationalbibliografie; detailed bibliographic data is available on the Internet at
<http://dnb.d-nb.de>.

1st edition May 2007

Editorial Office: Maria Akhavan-Hezavei

Gabler is a company of Springer Science+Business Media.
www.gabler.de

Cover design: Nina Faber de.sign, Wiesbaden
Setting: ITS Text und Satz Anne Fuchs, Bamberg
Printing and binding: Wilhelm & Adam, Heusenstamm
Printed on acid-free paper
Printed in Germany

ISBN 978-3-8349-0130-9

Contents

1 Communicating with clarity

It is vital when communicating, whether speaking or writing, that the message is clear and unambiguous and that your audience easily understands what you want to say. The best-practice guidelines that follow will help you to write effectively, to leave concise voicemails, and to make telephone calls with impact.

Writing clearly

Good writing comes from clear thinking. Both result from a clear message that a reader can immediately understand.

General Approach

- match the style to the reader
- use everyday English
- explain new ideas clearly

Phrasing and sentences

- avoid jargon e.g., Boolean logic (Internet usage)
- avoid clichés e.g., "there's no such thing as a free lunch"
- keep sentences and paragraphs short

Words

- use short words
- avoid pomposity e.g., not "I will endeavour to find out" but "I'll try to find out"
- avoid tautology (repetition using two or more words with the same meaning) e.g., not "the round glass globes" but "the glass globes"
- deal with the concrete rather than the abstract e.g., not "what means of transportation conveys you to work" but "how do you get to work – by car or by train?"
- use active rather than passive verbs

Use short sentences

Long sentences are usually complex sentences. They are difficult for the reader to digest. Try to keep your sentences as short as you can without making them disjointed.

A useful guide is to keep to one idea per sentence. If your average sentence length is below 25 words, you are probably writing concisely.

One definition of a sentence is that it must make COMPLETE sense.

Sentence and meaning

■ Task 1

Read the following sentences. If a sentence makes sense, tick ✓ the Sense column, if it does not make sense, tick ✓ the NonSense column. A sentence may not make sense because of its grammar. The first one has been done as an example.

Sentences	Sense	NonSense
1. He cooked the tomatoes in lubrication oil.		✓
2. All the tomatoes burst.		
3. The tomatoes, although he had cooked them with great care and had pricked them with a fork before putting them under the grill.		
4. Hissed and spluttered merrily in the bubbling oil.		
5. The tomatoes were fresh.		
6. Were the tomatoes fresh enough?		
7. What amazing tomatoes they were!		
8. With reference to the tomatoes received on July 2 20XX.		
9. The full details of our TOMATO SPECIAL including discounts for cash sales.		
10. Look forward to receiving your order for tomatoes in the very near future.		

■ Task 2

This sentence is over-long, over-complex, and incomprehensible. Rewrite it so that it makes sense.

Although no one seems to recall who coined the phrase Publish or Perish to describe the assertion that a university or even college teacher will not be promoted within the system of American higher education unless he conducts original research and proves his capabilities by publishing, the words have provided scholars and their publishers with an unparalleled opportunity to defend the faith.

Writing a good paragraph

Good paragraphs usually contain a topic sentence, supporting sentences, and a closing sentence. A topic sentence is usually the first sentence in a paragraph which introduces the main idea. Supporting sentences come after the topic sentence and develop the main idea. A closing sentence restates the main idea of the paragraph using different words.

Example

There are three reasons why New Zealand is one of the best countries to live in. First, New Zealand has an excellent healthcare system and all New Zealanders have access to medical services at a reasonable price. Second, New Zealand has a high standard of education. Students are taught by well-trained teachers and are encouraged to go on to higher education. Finally, New Zealand's cities are clean and efficiently managed with many parks and open spaces. New Zealanders generally are very environmentally aware. As a result, New Zealand is a desirable place to live.

■ Task 3

Construct a paragraph containing a topic sentence, supporting sentences, and a closing sentence from this information.

Exercise is good for you – everyone should exercise – it keeps you fit and healthy and reduces stress – it can help you keep your weight down, relieve depression, and is good for your heart

Effective paragraphing and linking

Paragraphs enable readers to see divisions within a document, making a smooth transition between topics. If a topic is lengthy or you have to, for example, present advantages and disadvantages or alternatives etc., you may need to subdivide the topic into more than one paragraph. The important thing is to limit paragraphs to a single topic or idea.

The length of the paragraphs should not, in general, exceed 175 words and will mostly consist of three to six sentences.

Most readers, unless they are academics, have difficulty reading continuous text, therefore using shorter paragraphs will make your message easier to understand.

The factual paragraph is often shorter than the explanatory paragraph as the latter may contain examples. A paragraph may consist of only a single sentence to emphasize important material. However, they should be used with care as too many single-sentence paragraphs can make your communication as hard to understand as if you'd used several very long paragraphs.

The structure of ideas within the paragraph should be logical. This could be:

- chronological
- problem to solution
- cause to effect
- general to specific
- important to less important etc.

Linking words/expressions

Example memo

When the XYZ system was first introduced, it was found to be both flexible and advanced. Moreover, its speed of operation was greater than comparable hardware then available. However, in recent months major faults have developed in the equipment, and the local agent appears incapable of providing a reliable repair service. Consequently, the system is regularly out of order for several days at a time.

Although the manufacturers have agreed to replace the system free of charge, the new equipment will not be installed for at least six months. Such a delay is clearly unacceptable to us. We should, therefore, insist that XYZ send their own engineer to upgrade the equipment. Alternatively, the equipment should be transported to the XYZ plant for inspection and repair there.

This memo is coherent because the ideas have been linked together with a series of linking words. If you eliminate these, you will find that the flow of ideas is lost.

■ Task 4

Look at the following sentences and link them, as in the example above, to develop a more coherent text.

Please refer to Appendix A on page 157 for a comprehensive overview of linking words and expressions.

Memo from: HR Manager
Date: 5ᵗʰ March 20XX

To: Managing Director
Ref: GHL/13/PO

(1) .... we have agreed in principle to try and cut down on staff, there are two serious problems in R&D.

(2) ...., the person in charge of ordering from the stores is also responsible for updating the database. (3) ...., at the end of the month, when most people want replacements from the stores, and (4) .... require information from the database, he is unable to perform both tasks quickly enough. (5) ...., he is practically unoccupied during the first week of every month, when he could be helping someone else, (6) .... I suggest we try to reorganise his job to improve efficiency.

*(7) ...., the administrative secretary has got rather set in her ways, and (8) ....,
is still refusing to use the new software. I (9) .... recommend that she should be
invited to retire early, (10) .... we will have complete chaos as far as record keeping
is concerned. If we were to appoint a more flexible and better trained secretary to
replace her, there would be several advantages over the present arrangements. (11)
.............., we could put her in charge of updating all the information in the department
and (12) .... reduce the burden on the person in charge of ordering from the stores.
We might (13) .... ask her to take a more active part in producing the annual report
for R&D than her predecessor has done.*

*(14) ...., I would argue that we approach the appropriate union, and suggest that
the present administrative secretary should be retired early and, (15) ...., that her
job should be upgraded to Grade 2. (16) .... I would be prepared to draw up a new
job description pending your agreement.*

Telephoning in English

Leaving a voicemail

Hints on voicemail organisation:

▶ top down not bottom up e.g., give the main message but don't supply all the details
▶ content not process
▶ synthesis not summary e.g., state what the message is and the actions you'd like the
other person to take

Tips on leaving a voicemail:

▶ no longer than 60 seconds
▶ summarise the purpose of your message in a sentence or two
▶ give your name and telephone number early in the message
▶ speak slowly and distinctly
▶ give the recipient enough information to act
▶ say when you will be able to receive a return call

Leaving a message in your own voicemail:

▶ give your name clearly
▶ say when you will be available to receive a call
▶ do not say 'speak after the tone'
▶ do not say 'you have reached the voicemail of ...' – we all have enough experience
of using the telephone and leaving messages!

Expressions you can use when you leave a voicemail:

Starting the message	Hello, this is ....
Saying the day/time you are leaving the message	It's Tuesday June 10 It's 10 a.m.
Giving the reason for your call	I urgently need to talk to you about ....
Leaving your number	Please call me back on .... I will be in the office until ....

■ Task 5

Leave a voicemail in the following situations:

1. *Your boss has a meeting arranged at 9 a.m. tomorrow morning (Thursday) with Mr Smith but he has just called you to tell you that he is held up in Italy and has asked you to ring to cancel the meeting and make another appointment. He will be available Friday afternoon and then not until Tuesday of the next week. Leave a voicemail for Mr Smith. Jot down what you are going to say in the call.*

2. *You are arranging a conference call between your boss and Mr Wang in Taiwan. Ring Mr Wang's PA and leave her a voicemail asking at what time GMT it would suit Mr Wang to receive a call from your boss. Jot down what you are going to say in the call.*

Arranging a meeting

The scenario:

You work as PA to Karl Braun, the European marketing director of MicroX, a US software company which has its European headquarters in Munich. Your boss reports to the marketing director in the US. MicroX has 15 subsidiaries all over Europe and marketing meetings for all European marketing managers are held monthly in Munich. However, your boss has received an email from Clara Sullivan, the marketing director in the US HQ in Texas, asking him to change the venue of the next marketing meeting from Munich to Rome as accommodation costs are cheaper there. Clara thinks it would be good to rotate the venue of the monthly marketing meetings throughout the European subsidiaries and preferably to cheaper locations than Munich. She would also like to attend the next European marketing meeting. You have already emailed all the marketing managers informing them of the change of venue – some were very happy about it but others less so, especially Ana Ribero from Madrid who left you this message:

"This is Ana Ribero from MicroX Madrid. About the meeting in Rome, I think this is a bad idea as it will cut heavily into my working time and I will still have to come to Munich anyhow to talk to my colleagues in R&D – so let's keep the venue in Munich as usual."

Karl Braun, your boss, has asked you to phone Ana on his behalf to inform her that the meeting will take place in Rome and to persuade her to come. Before you make the call, plan your strategy:

➤ is it a good idea to mention that the change of venue is Clara's idea?

➤ what advantages can you present to her for having the meeting in Rome? For example, it's a good idea to visit other European subsidiaries; accommodation costs are cheaper; perhaps the next meeting could be held in Madrid etc.

➤ you could offer to help her with her travel arrangements

➤ perhaps you could send her any important information she needs from R&D

■ Task 6

Jot down what you are going to say in the call. Here are some expressions you can use to help you with the call.

Stage	Marker	Expression
Identification	Ah, Hello.	This is ... Is that ...?
Preliminaries	Mr, X George ...	How are things in (Madrid)? What's the weather like?
Business	Listen, Mr Y Look,	I'm calling about... I wonder if you can help me? I've got a bit of a problem with ...
Summary	So, just to confirm then ... So, let's sum up ...	I'll send you ... I'll meet you at ...
Check	OK? Alright then?	
Termination	Good. Well ... Goodbye then.	I look forward to hearing from you/ seeing you on ...

You have phoned Ana and she has agreed to come to Rome – she is not happy about it but you were sufficiently persuasive. Then you receive a voicemail from Clara Sullivan:

"This is Clara Sullivan from MicroX, Texas. I'm calling about the meeting in Rome next week. It's got to be in Oslo not Rome because I have another meeting scheduled in Oslo. Could you let your people know please?"

That's put the cat amongst the pigeons – several managers are already unhappy about going to Rome and now they will have to be told at this late date that the location has been changed yet again. Karl Braun, your boss, hands you this email – his English is not great – and asks you to put it into good English and send it off to the marketing managers.

You know that your boss is sometimes over-direct in his approach to people and that you will need to rewrite his draft in a more diplomatic and tactful style.

■ Task 7

Using your boss's draft below, produce an improved version of his email. You can leave out or add information as well as amend the text, if you feel it is necessary.

Email:

To: Mr X, Marketing Manager
From: Karl Braun, European Marketing Manager
Subject: changing the meeting again

We have to change the venue of the next meeting from Rome to Oslo.

So please ignore yesterday's email. The reason of the change is that Clara Sullivan has a meeting in Oslo on the same day. So it's convenient for her to join us at the meeting. Meeting her is very useful for us all so we are very pleased by this.

Sorry about this confusion, but the new plan is for the best.

I or my Personal Assistant will call you in the next few days to discuss about the meeting. Please be ready with any special requests you have in connection with the agenda.

We will be here to help you with any problems with travel arrangements.

Sorry again!

Regards

Karl Braun

Set business phrases

Here are expressions you can use to help you write the email. They can also be used in business letters.

References

Thank you for your email of ...
Further to our telephone conversation yesterday ...

Requests

We should be grateful if you would/could ...
Would you be so kind as to ...
We should appreciate it if you could ...
Could you please ...
Would you mind ...-ing ...
Please let me know when/how much/if

Expressing urgency and necessity

... as soon as you possibly can
I am sure you will realise that
It is essential that ...

Expressing willingness and offers to help

We are/should be (quite) prepared to ...
We should be willing to ...
Would you like us to ...
Please do not hesitate to get in touch with us if we can be of any (further) assistance/if you need any (further) information ...

Making suggestions and proposals

Might/May we suggest that ...
One possible solution would be to ...
We propose to ...
We are planning to ...

Asking for approval

We (sincerely) hope/trust that ... will be to your satisfaction/meet with your approval.
We hope/trust that you will have no objections/be agreeable to ...
Would you have any objection if ...

Confirmation

May I confirm the arrangements for/that ...
Would you please confirm that ...
Please drop us a line if ... (informal).

2 Best-practice emails and working in multi-cultural teams

Email is rapidly overtaking letter writing as the most common form of written communication. We tend to transfer our communication style from our native language to a foreign language. This can throw up cross-cultural issues as email is an instant form of communication and is often far less formal stylistically than writing a letter. For example, if we forget to maintain the relationship by just getting straight down to business, we can alienate the person we are corresponding with. However, email has many advantages.

Advantages of emails

- eliminates phone tag (people out)
- allows you to put more time and thought into messages than when phoning
- breaks down distance/time barriers
- shortens cycle of written communication
- allows for more direct/interactive communication
- improves productivity e.g., meeting planning and preparation
- reduces telephone interruptions
- allows people to work from any location with a computer

However, there are also distinct traps you can fall into if you don't observe some simple rules. As with letters or faxes, emails can be misinterpreted since there is no body language or voice tone to enable the reader to pick up clues. The easiest way to check if your email is appropriate or not is to ask yourself how you would feel if you received it. Below are the ten most common mistakes people make when they write emails and tips on how to avoid them.

Dos and don'ts

1. No clear subject title. The subject line should be clear and concise. It should not contain negative words or expressions.

2. No greeting. Always begin your email with a friendly greeting.

3. Too many abbreviations and acronyms. Don't pepper your email with abbreviations and acronyms – they can be misunderstood and misinterpreted as being rude or demanding.

4. Copying in too many other people. Don't cc others unless they are directly involved in the situation otherwise you just add to the spam that we all receive on a daily basis.

5. Too many mistakes. Pay attention to your spelling, punctuation, and grammar. Writing an email full of mistakes reduces your credibility with your reader.

6. Flaming. Writing an email in capital letters to make a point is annoying to read. In any case, you should never send an email when you're angry – it's the equivalent of throwing a wobbler in cyberspace – just sit on it for a bit till you've calmed down. Equally, you should also never write an email all in lower case.

7. No closing or signing off. You should always sign off in a friendly way and try to end on a positive note.

8. Difficult to read. Long emails with no attention to paragraphing, sentence structure, or unnecessary repetition are difficult to both read and understand. You run the risk of your reader hitting the delete button.

9. Unfriendly tone. If you have to deal with a delicate situation by email, you do yourself no favours by sounding aggressive or downright hostile. You will immediately put the reader on the defensive and are unlikely to get a helpful response.

10. General lack of clarity. Make sure that your reader knows what you expect them to do in response to your email. Convey your message clearly and concisely.

■ Task 1

Match the bodies of emails 1 – 4 with their responses A – D. N.B. They all break the rules of best practice in one way or another.

1. *I tried to call you but, as usual, you weren't there. I've just had the production manager from Makro on the phone – he's absolutely livid about the late delivery and is going to switch from us to another supplier. Due to your incompetence, we're going to lose the best customer we've ever had.*

2. *The meeting has been arranged for Tuesday next week at 11 a.m. in the Green Room. The whole department is expected to attend as there is going to be an important announcement.*
   Look forward to seeing you there.

3. *FYI the alarms are going to be tested next Monday @ 8. FWIW it'll only last 5 mins and BTW this is going to happen on a weekly basis.*
   TTFN.

4. *Just heard a really juicy piece of gossip – do you remember Peter Brown – well I hear he's about to be sacked. Great isn't it? He's such a pain.*
    Look forward to seeing you at the conference and don't forget to bring the presentation on team building with you.

A. *Thanks for the info. Did you know he's my brother-in-law? He'll be thrilled at the news.*
    See you at the conference with the presentation.

B. *COULDN'T TAKE YOUR CALL COS I WAS SORTING OUT THE S*** WE'RE IN. HAVE MANAGED TO SALVAGE THE SITUATION WITH NO THANKS TO YOU.*

C. *Thanx got the info 6 times. I already knew anyhow.*

D. *About the meeting on Tuesday next week – well I know I should go but, you know how it is – I've got all behind with my work – and what I really want to know is – do I have to go or could I, just for once, like you know skip it.*

■ **Task 2**

Have a look back at best practice for writing emails and then note down what mistakes the authors have made.

■ **Task 3**

Give a one-line summary in polite English of the real message in each. (1 – 4 & A – D).

Common abbreviations

Of course, when we're emailing friends we do use abbreviations, acronyms, and emoticons. Here are a few of the most common with their meanings but use them with care.

ABBREVIATION	TERM
aka	also known as
a.m.	ante meridiem (morning)
approx	approximately
et al	et alia (and others)
etc	et cetera (and so forth)
ASAP	as soon as possible
Bcc	blind copy carbon
bldg	building
CY	calendar year
cc	carbon copy to
COD	cash on delivery
COLA	cost of living adjustment
Co.	company

Corp.	corporation
Dept.	department
dba	doing business as
ea.	each
e.o.m.	end of month
FY	fiscal year
e.g.	exempli gratia (for example)
FYI	for your information
govt.	government
Inc.	incorporated
IOU	I owe you
Ltd.	limited
mfg,	manufacturing
mdse.	merchandise
mo.	month
viz.	videlicet (namely)
no.	numero (number)
p.m.	post merediem (afternoon)
PS	postscript
qtr.	quarter
VIP	very important person

Common e-mail acronyms

ACRONYM	EXPRESSION
BRB	be right back
BTW	by the way
CUL	see you later
F2F	face to face
FWIW	for what it's worth
FYA	for your amusement
GD&R	grinning, ducking and running
GMTA	great minds think alike
HHOK	ha ha only kidding
IMHO	in my humble opinion
IOW	in other words
LOL	laughing out loud
OBTW	oh, by the way
OIC	oh, I see
ROFL	rolling on the floor laughing
SO	significant other (partner/spouse)
TIA	thanks in advance

TNX	thanks
TTFN	ta-ta (bye) for now
WB	welcome back
WRT	with respect to
WTG	way to go

Emoticons or Smilies

SMILEY	EMOTION	SMILEY	EMOTION
:-)	happy	:-[	sad sarcasm
:-(	sad	;-(	feel like crying
:-&	tongue-tied	:'-(	crying
:-<	really upset	%-)	happy confused
:-| |	angry	%-(	sad confused
:-(O)	yelling	:-*	kiss
:-D	laughing	:-\	undecided
;-)	winking	:-✐	my lips are sealed
8-)	wide-eyed	8-O	shocked
:-|	apathetic	:-}	grinning
:-o	amazed	:-/	puzzled
:-	sarcastic smile	X-(	brain dead (over-tired)
O:-)	angelic	:-P	sticking tongue out

To email or not from your work computer

■ **Task 4**

Look at the situations below – for which ones could you send an email from your work computer?

1. *You've heard an embarrassing story about a colleague you dislike.*

2. *You urgently need a report from a colleague – you've reminded her once but she still hasn't sent it.*

3. *You want to change the time and date of a business meeting.*

4. *You were supposed to send out an agenda for tomorrow's meeting but you forgot to.*

5.   *Your cat's had 6 kittens and you'd like to find a kind and loving home for them.*

6.   *Your junior colleague didn't do a very good job organising a conference – you want to give her some feedback.*

Giving negative feedback by email

Generally, we don't write emails giving negative feedback but sometimes we find ourselves in the situation where we have to – especially to service providers such as hotels, travel agents etc.

■ Task 5

Write an email giving negative feedback to the hotel.

Last week a visitor to your company stayed in a hotel that you booked and your company paid for. When the visitor is about to leave, they tell you that the service in the hotel was appalling – their toilet didn't function for two days out of the three they stayed there, room service took ages to arrive and when it did the food was cold, and although the hotel reassured you that there was Internet access in all the bedrooms, it didn't function.

Here are some expressions you can use:

▶   *We regret to inform you ...*
▶   *We were not satisfied with ...*
▶   *We find this unacceptable ...*
▶   *It was a serious inconvenience ...*
▶   *We are sure we can come to a mutually acceptable agreement ...*

Working in multi-cultural teams

Nowadays, we are increasingly working in multi-cultural teams which bring with them, their own specific challenges.

■ Task 6

As you read the article below on working in multi-cultural teams, find words/ expressions which have the same meaning as:

1.   *use*
2.   *variety*
3.   *problems*
4.   *maintaining*
5.   *incorrect interpretations*
6.   *representation of something as less than it really is*

7. *to be open about*
8. *things which are awaited*
9. *essential*
10. *continuous*

The Challenges of Multi-Cultural Teamwork

For the international secretary and PA, working in multi-cultural teams is driven by the need to coordinate the activities of highly mobile managers who often divide their working time between different international locations. It is also driven by the need to organise international events – such as conferences, meetings, and PR events – involving the participation of a number of local offices.

The advantages of multi-cultural teams are clear. The opportunity to bring 'local' perspectives and knowledge to support 'global' initiatives and draw on the best talent and skills (regardless of where they are located) helps companies to find the optimum processes and solutions for their international activities. However, while multi-cultural teams help companies to adapt more effectively to the new global business environment, they can carry problems of 'internal integration'. Diversity of background and perspective among team members brings special challenges, such as the creation and development of trust, a sense of common purpose and identity, and an ability to communicate and make effective decisions. As teams of support staff are often less mobile than the managers they serve, there is normally the additional challenge of working together at a distance and relying on remote technology as a medium of communication and integration.

A key issue that affects the work of the international secretary or PA is communication. How direct should they be in communicating sensitive issues via email? In some cultures, effective communication is more about saying clearly what you mean, keeping it short and simple, and communicating feedback explicitly. In other cultures, effective communication is more about servicing relationships and communicating things indirectly, particularly when someone's 'face' is at stake. Such differences in style and attitude often lead to misunderstandings, particularly when communicating mainly by email and with limited opportunities to get to know each other.

For example, a British PA's email comment that 'We might need more support on the conference organisation' may not be given the attention it deserves by her German counterpart due to a lack of awareness of the British tendency to use understatement as a way of signalling problems. Clearly, in order to integrate multi-cultural teams, there is a need to bring to the surface differing expectations about the most effective way of communicating and working together and, at a distance, this can be difficult to achieve.

Working at a distance, and relying on remote communication media (such as email and telephone) poses special challenges for multi-cultural teams of assistants and PAs. If team members are rarely out of their cultural space, it becomes harder to understand the motives and priorities of their colleagues in distant contexts. Trust is difficult to build and easier to lose when there are no opportunities to 'rub shoulders' and drink coffee with teammates. Loyalties to the team may be less compelling than loyalties to the local office. The importance of effective integration at the start-up phase of teamwork is important for all kinds of multi-cultural teams, as it creates the basis for ongoing personal relationships, trust, and mutual understanding. The added challenge for teams of international secretaries is that they don't often get the opportunity to start by meeting face-to-face. This puts an extra pressure on the quality of their interpersonal sensitivity and communication skills, as well as the appropriacy of the choices they make in selecting and optimising communication media – including how and when to use email, phone, tele- and video-conferencing. Here, an understanding is required of the 'added-value' potential of telephone over email in overcoming potential misunderstandings, confirming understanding, and handling conflict. International secretaries can play a vital part in ensuring that their approach to communication with their counterparts across cultures is far more strategic in vision than just focusing on reacting to the ever-flowing stream of emails in their inboxes.

(adapted from an article by Nigel Ewington, first published in working@office)

■ Task 7

With reference to the article and drawing on your own experience, answer these questions.

1. *Why did the British PA's email not receive the attention it needed?*

2. *How can this sort of misunderstanding be overcome?*

3. *Why could the telephone be a more effective method of communication than an email?*

Raising awareness of different communication styles

As you can see from the information in the article above, Germans tend to be more direct in their communication style than other nationalities, for example, the British who favour a more indirect style. Have a look at the cline on the next page:

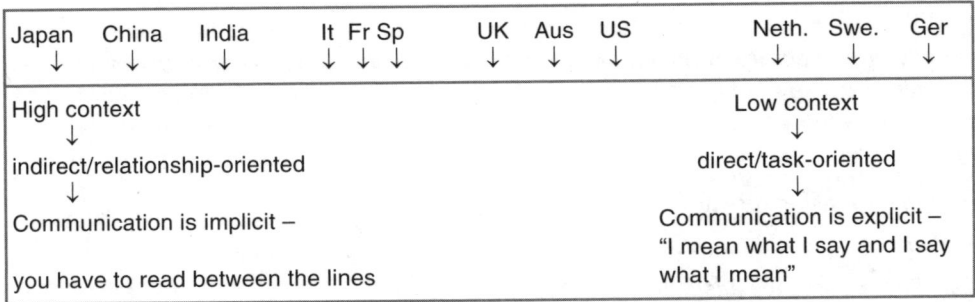

Japan	China	India		It Fr Sp		UK	Aus	US		Neth.	Swe.	Ger
↓	↓	↓		↓ ↓ ↓		↓	↓	↓		↓	↓	↓

High context	Low context
↓	↓
indirect/relationship-oriented	direct/task-oriented
↓	↓
Communication is implicit –	Communication is explicit – "I mean what I say and I say what I mean"
you have to read between the lines	

Adapted from Edward Hall

We can see that the Chinese/Japanese are at one end of the scale with the Germans/Scandinavians at the other end and with the UK/US more or less towards the middle. As we all have different communication preferences, it is worth bearing this in mind when communicating with different nationalities.

■ Task 8

You receive this voicemail from a Chinese colleague in the Shanghai branch. You are both attending the same international conference with your bosses in a couple of weeks.

Hello, this is Clementine Liu from the Shanghai office. How are you? I wonder if I could trouble you? I have a bit of a problem with the PowerPoint charts that I need to prepare. I'd be very grateful if you could help me with the text for them because your written English is much better than mine. I'll call you back tomorrow morning at 9 am your time if that's convenient. Thank you and have a good evening.

You have a lot of work and could really do without any more to do. However, you are willing to lend her a hand. She is about to give you a ring – remember that the Chinese are very relationship-oriented, so be prepared to engage in small talk before getting to the point of the call and don't let her lose face. Complete your part of the conversation.

CL: *Hello, this is Clementine Liu from the Shanghai office. How are you?*

1. You: ....

CL: *I'm fine too thank you and how's the weather?*

2. You: ....

CL: *It's quite humid here but luckily we have air conditioning. How was your holiday?*

3. You: ....

CL: *Oh good! It's very nice to talk to you again. I was just wondering if you got my voicemail?*

4. *You:* ....

CL: *I've got a bit of a problem as I said. Do you think you would have the time to just check my charts for me?*

5. *You:* ....

CL: *That would be great. Thank you so much, I'll email them through to you and I'm really looking forward to seeing you again.*

6. *You:* ....

CL: *Thank you once again and goodbye.*

■ Task 9

When you get to the office on Monday morning, you find that you received this voicemail from a US PA the previous Friday evening.

Hi, this is Claire speaking from XYZ company in Seattle. About the meeting in Munich next week, do you think we could kick off at 10 instead of 8? And could you push lunch back to 1.30? The reason is that Mr A is taking a different flight which will arrive pretty late in the evening and he'd therefore like to start a bit later in the morning so that he can get some shuteye. Can you let me know asap please?

This is going to be difficult for you to arrange as there are several other meeting participants. However, Mr A is an important participant so you'd like to help him. The best you can do, without upsetting others' schedules, is to change the start of the meeting to 9 am and break for lunch at 12.30. You pick up the phone to leave her a message but before you do, reflect on what you know of the preferred communication style of Americans.

Here's how you can order your voicemail:

▶ ask her how she is
▶ get down to business
▶ suggest a compromise solution
▶ sign off

Here are some expressions you can use:

Maintaining the relationship

▶ Hi, how are you?
▶ How nice to hear from you
▶ How are things your end?

Getting down to business

▶ I'm returning your call about ...
▶ I gather there's a problem with ...
▶ I understand ... is going to be ...

Suggesting a compromise

▶ What if we ...
▶ How about if we ...
▶ If we ..., would that help?

Signing off

▶ It'd be good to hear from you soon
▶ It'd be nice to talk to you so that we can ...
▶ Let me know if there's anything else I can do

Now write down what you'd say:

. . . .

. . . .

. . . .

. . . .

. . . .

. . . .

Next time you have to deal with someone from a different culture whether on the phone, face-to-face, or by email, it's a good idea to reflect on what you know about that culture. Therefore, don't be surprised if your Italian counterpart likes to chat a bit before getting down to business or if your Dutch colleague gets straight to the point. Neither style is better – they're just different!

3 Building business relationships

Striking up a conversation with someone you don't know very well can be difficult as you're not always sure what topics are appropriate to talk about. But building rapport is an essential part of establishing and maintaining relationships, which, in turn, are essential elements of doing business successfully in a global environment.

■ Task 1

Read the article 'Small Talk – Big Problem' and find words or phrases which mean:

1. a person who takes part in a conversation, dialogue or discussion
2. makes easier
3. to start immediately
4. carry out successfully
5. promotes/builds
6. bounces
7. to widen
8. rejecting
9. involved in
10. instrument

Small Talk – Big Problem

Small talk is a vitally important function of the English language because it helps you to build a relationship with your interlocutor. It facilitates international relations at every level. Look, for example, at the level of understanding the Blairs had with the Clintons – they certainly didn't just speak about politics.

Why is small talk a big problem? Germans are a low-context culture which means they are task-oriented and not used to small talk, preferring to get straight down to business. To other nationalities this can make them seem unfriendly, particularly those from higher context cultures such as the British and the Latins. These cultures are relationship-oriented and they like and expect to exchange a few words before they get down to business.

Why make small talk at all?

You may ask, 'what is the point of small talk?' – you don't achieve anything and it wastes time. On the contrary – small talk enables you to build a bridge with your interlocutor and to move quickly from 'I' and 'they' to a feeling of 'we'. Finding common ground fosters trust and enables you to build relationships with people from other cultures.

Of course you can't just talk about anything – you should avoid personal and hot topics such as sex, politics, religion, and money. These topics, as in any other cultures, you reserve for close friends.

Be an active listener

Making small talk is a bit like playing table tennis – the conversational ball pingpongs back and forth. You also mustn't forget that to build rapport you need to be a sympathetic listener. Although 'mm mm' and 'yes' are acceptable, try to broaden your range of active listening devices as too much use of 'mm mm' can sound dismissive and as if you're really bored. Experiment with using 'oh really?', 'that's interesting', 'I see' etc. and sound as though you really mean it. This shows your partner that you're engaged in the dialogue and really listening to what they're saying.

Small talk is a bridge to building a relationship and is just another tool in your linguistic toolbox, like grammar or vocabulary. Language is about communicating but don't forget that you will always be communicating with a person and not a robot. This is why small talk is very important as it shows your interlocutor that you are interested in them as a person.

Making small talk

When you meet someone for the first time, you need to introduce yourself.

Introducing yourself

A: *I'm Elke Schmidt. How do you do?*
B: *I'm Ramona Braun. How do you do?*
A: *Pleased to meet you.*
B: *Nice to meet you too.*

This is a standard formulaic exchange. If you've met the person before, you can say:

A: *How nice to see you again/How are you?/ How are things?*
B: *Good to see you too?/Very well and you?/Great and what about you?*

When you meet someone in a social situation, it's useful to have communication techniques that move quickly from a sense of "us and them" to a feeling of "we."

■ Task 2

Look at the following exchanges to establish common interest and classify them according to:

a) likes/dislikes
b) opinions
c) experience

1. A: *I think the Harry Potter books are overrated.*
   B: *I think so too.*

2. A: *I've visited the USA a number of times.*
   B: *Really? So have I? Where did you go?.*

3. A: *I really like modern art.*
   B: *Yes, I do too.*

4. A: *I can't stand in-flight food.*
   B: *I can't either.*

5. A: *Creativity is the key word.*
   B: *I couldn't agree more.*

6. A: *I worked in marketing for a number of years.*
   B: *That's interesting. So did I. What did you do exactly?*

Building on small talk

As you will usually get an answer linked to what you've said, you can then build on it to establish rapport.

For example:

A: *So what do you think of Frankfurt?*

B: *Well, I don't know Frankfurt so well but I like big cities in general.*

A: *Me too. Well, I was actually born here so I guess it's in my blood. Where do you come from originally?*

B: *I'm from New York originally. Have you ever been there?*

A: *Yes, I've been there many times and I really like it. It's got this buzz to it.*

■ Task 3

You've just met someone at a conference who tells you they're from London. How would you continue the conversation?

A: *I'm from London – do you know the city?*
You: *(say you visited last year and where you went)*
A: *What did you think of London?*
You: *(give an opinion and talk about something you liked)*

Safe topics to talk about

When you're making small talk, it's best to stick to neutral topics to avoid potentially offending your interlocutor.

■ Task 4

Look at the following comments and decide whether they are "safe" (S) or a bit "risky" (R).

1. *Isn't it a lovely day?*
2. *How much do you earn?*
3. *How old are you?*
4. *How was your journey?*
5. *Have you been here before?*
6. *I go to church every Sunday? What about you?*
7. *I think the Social Democrats are the only party with the right ideas.*
8. *I had a terrible journey here.*
9. *Are you married?*
10. *When are you going to get a new job?*

■ Task 5

A visitor you've never met has just arrived at your office. She has an appointment with you. What do you say?

You: *((1) greet her and introduce yourself)*
Visitor: *Good morning. I'm Annie Brown from Legasystems, Birmingham. How do you do?*
You: *((2) respond)*
Visitor: *Pleased to meet you too.*
You: *((3) offer some refreshment and make some small talk before getting down to business)*

Use open questions when you make small talk

It's best to avoid asking closed questions that can be answered by a monosyllabic "yes" or "no." Compare the two dialogues below:

Dialogue 1

A: Is this your first trip to Germany?
B: Yes, it is.
A: Did you have a good flight?
B: Yes, I did.
A: Is your hotel comfortable?
B: Yes, it is.

Dialogue 2

A: Is this your first trip to Germany?
B: Yes, it is.
A: How do you find it?
B: Heidelberg is a beautiful city. It reminds me of Cambridge which is also an old university city.
A: Which part are you staying in?
B: I'm in the old part – right in the middle of the pedestrian zone in a beautiful old hotel.
A: How is the hotel – I hope it's comfortable?
B: It's an old coaching inn and it's very atmospheric with beams everywhere and some lovely antiques. I also have a really comfortable room, thank you, and very quiet too so I got a good night's sleep.

The first dialogue might make your visitor feel a little uncomfortable as all the questions can be answered in one or two words. However, the second dialogue opens up the conversation far more and starts to build rapport.

■ Task 6

You've met someone at a seminar and you want to find out more about what they do and why they're there. Ask a few open questions to get the information.

Active listening

Engaging in a conversation is two-way traffic and each person shares responsibility to make it a pleasant experience and to keep it going. Unlike many other languages, English has a wide range of minimal responses which show your interlocutor that you're listening. It's especially important to use them when you're on the telephone – the worst thing that can happen, and it's happened to all of us, is when the other person says, "Are you still there?"

Minimal responses

Responding to neutral information or to good news:

▶ Right, yes
▶ I follow you
▶ I'm with you
▶ That's great!
▶ Good!

Responding to bad news:

▶ Oh, no!
▶ That's terrible!
▶ Oh dear!
▶ I'm so sorry
▶ What a shame!

■ Task 7

Use appropriate active listening expressions to respond to these sentences.

1. *I've got a terrible headache.*

2. *I've just been promoted and what it means is not only more money but ...*

3. *If we implement the new strategy, the company would break even by year end and ...*

4. *I've just heard that we're downsizing and lots of people are going to lose their jobs.*

5. *If you want to write notes on the bottom of a chart, what you have to do is ...*

6. *I got stuck in a horrendous traffic jam on the way home last night.*

7. *I hear that our Christmas bonus is going to be really generous this year.*

8. *My plane had a 3-hour delay.*

9. *There was an accident on the motorway this morning and all the participants are going to be late for the meeting.*

10. *I've just spilt coffee all over my work.*

Helping a corporate visitor with problems

Often we need to help a visitor if they have problems or need something done urgently.

Here are some expressions you can use to respond to requests for help:

May I ....
Can I ....
Shall I .... (for you)
Could I ....
Would you like (me to) ....
I can .... for you, if you'd like me to

■ Task 8

Respond to these requests for help:

1.   *I need to send a fax urgently.*
2.   *I've lost my credit cards. Could you help me please?*
3.   *I need a taxi to the airport immediately otherwise I'll miss my flight.*

■ Task 9

A visitor to your company arrives soaking wet for an appointment. You offer to help. What do you say?

1.   ....

2.   ....

3.   ....

4.   ....

Writing an email to a new acquaintance – formality vs informality

Last week you attended a conference where you met an English PA, Pamela Hutchinson. You got on very well with her and you'd really like to keep in touch. So, on your return, you decide to write her an email. Unfortunately, the emails you usually write are very formal and so you ask an English colleague to have a look at what you've written below.

From: ....
To: Pamela Hutchinson
Subject: Conference September 14 – 16, 20XX
Dear Ms Hutchinson, It was a great pleasure to meet you at the conference from September 14 – 16, 20XX. I very much enjoyed our conversation and would be delighted to have the opportunity to renew our acquaintanceship. You mentioned that you might be visiting Germany in the near future. If so, I would be delighted to act as your guide. I very much look forward to hearing from you again. Yours sincerely .... PA to Ms Z

■ **Task 10**

Your English colleague tells you that, as you feared, your email is far too formal. Write it again using more informal expressions.

Here are some informal expressions you can use:

STARTING	BODY OF THE EMAIL
Hi	I really enjoyed ....
Dear	It was so nice to ....
	I'd like to ....
	It'd be great if we could ....
SIGNING OFF	**ENDING**
Please stay in touch	Regards
Look forward to hearing from you soon	Best regards
Hope to hear from you soon	All the best

You get this email back:

From: Pamela Hutchinson
To: ....
Subject: Coming to Germany
Dear .... It was great to get your email. In fact, great minds think alike, I was going to email you too but you got there first. I'm actually coming to Germany and right to your neck of the woods too next month. It'd be really nice to meet up and get to know each a bit better. Will you be around between Oct 17 – 19? Let me know what your plans are and then we can arrange to have dinner or something. All the best Pam

■ Task 11

Answer her email telling her you are around, you would like to meet her, and suggest a time and place.

From: ....
To:
Subject:
Dear

4 Delegating

Increasingly, we find ourselves trying to do too many tasks at the same time and consequently feeling frustrated that we never get to the end of our to-do list. The most effective way of remedying the situation is to delegate some of our work. This isn't, of course, always easy for the control freaks amongst us. Delegating shouldn't be seen as a negative but as a proactive solution.

Do you associate terms such as *letting go* with delegation, or is delegation something far more dynamic? Delegation is dynamic. It means work gets done through the process of the leader passing on authority and responsibility at the right time to the right people.

Know your team and the task requirements

As the leader of a team you will have assessed your team; you will already know their strengths and weaknesses as well as your own. When deciding who should do which tasks, the following areas should be considered:

▶ Where does the task fit functionally within the team? For example, if someone is already working on financial matters, would the new task fit into this existing area of work?

▶ Who has enough time and a workload which allows for additional tasks – or can some existing tasks be delegated to someone else?

▶ Who would be interested in taking on the new task?

▶ Who has the skill and experience required?

▶ Who would respond well to a new challenge?

▶ Who would you like to give this opportunity for development to?

WARNING: Leaders may be tempted to delegate to people who always say yes or those who always produce good work, and as a result, those people can become so overloaded that they find the situation unacceptably stressful. The workload needs to be spread evenly across the team.

You will need to start planning delegation as soon as you see work overload on the horizon. Analyse the workload, the time available, and earmark team members for additional or new tasks. This means you have to know exactly what the new tasks involve so that you can clearly communicate this to the team members.

Vocabulary

Words with *over*

In the paragraph on the previous page there is an example of a word with the prefix *over,* overload.

The prefix *over* has four main meanings:

▶ too much, e.g., overpopulation
▶ above, beyond, across, e.g., overhead telephone wires
▶ outer, e.g., overcoat
▶ additional, e.g., overtime

The phrase work overload, therefore, means too much work.

■ Task 1

Match the word or phrase to its definition. The first one has been done as an example.

Word or phrase with *over*		Definition
1. the overall cost	D	A. took more time than expected
2. an overbearing colleague		B. do something too extremely
3. go overboard		C. very worried/nervous/upset
4. overcome her shyness		D. including everything
5. This announcement is long overdue.		E. not notice
		F. too many people want it
6. The company became overextended financially.		G. successfully control a feeling/ emotion
7. an overhaul of the tax system		H. it is too much/difficult to deal with
8. Nobody could overlook the fact that sales were down.		I. domineering
		J. not made by the time expected
9. overriding consideration		K. detailed examination with the purpose of making improvements
10. The final speaker overran by half an hour.		
11. The seminar became oversubscribed.		L. more important than all others
12. overwhelmed with paperwork		M. borrowed more money than they could repay
13. overwrought		

Excellent communication skills

The person who you would like to take on the new tasks needs to be consulted. When the person has agreed to take on the new tasks, get this team member on board early on in all the discussions related to the tasks. In this way, they are well briefed and have the opportunity to influence the decisions made. This is often a good opportunity for the leader to point out the team member's strengths and to communicate the fact that, by delegating, the leader is recognising the abilities of the team member. It goes without saying that when delegating, a clear description of the task and clear instructions are vital. The type of language you use (formal/ neutral/ informal) and the tone you use (authoritative/negotiating) will depend on company culture, your relationship with the team member, and perhaps the nature of the task.

Expressions for getting something done

■ Task 2

Are the following expressions authoritative or negotiating in tone? Put A for authoritative or N for negotiating next to each one.

1. Do you think you could ...	6. It would be great if you could ...
2. I need you to deal with ...	7. I'm going to hand xxxxx over to you.
3. Would you mind ...	8. You're to see to it that ...
4. You'll have to ...	9. Now, what I want you to do is ...
5. Do you think you'd be able to ...	10. Could I ask you to ...

Sample sentences

▶ *Maria, could I ask you to take on responsibility for producing the quarterly sales report?*

▶ *Jack, I'll need you to deal with the increased number of client calls we're bound to get as a result of the advertising campaign.*

▶ *Do you think you'd be able to get your initial thoughts on this back to me by Friday, say?*

▶ *You're to see to it that we're getting the maximum discounts available on all our orders.*

■ **Task 3**

Write a sentence asking someone to do something for each of these scenarios. Think about which tone, negotiating or authoritative, would be suitable.

1.   *Eva must redraft the contract by the end of the day.*

2.   *You're not sure if Mark will be able to meet the visitors arriving at 10 pm.*

3.   *You wonder if Carla would like to take on the responsibility for organizing the conference in Geneva.*

4.   *It is essential that Tom contact all the people going to the 2 pm meeting to inform them of the room change.*

5.   *You're running out of time and hope that Emma can collate the seminar folders for you.*

Empowering and ongoing support

Delegating means giving a team member the authority necessary to carry out the task and when the team member accepts the responsibility, they become accountable to you for the outcome. When a team member becomes accountable for a task, the team leader, in turn, is responsible for supporting the team member with resources and training. Team members should have a sense of ownership of their new tasks and realise that they can influence some of the decision making in the company. Similarly, they realise that the leader trusts their professional judgment.

Support needs to be ongoing, for example, during work on a project, the team leader may have to:

1. review objectives
2. discuss actual and potential obstacles
3. clarify the task
4. elicit/give feedback
5. show appreciation
6. review resources required
7. review deadlines
8. ensure all lines of communication are open

Expressions for ongoing support

■ Task 4

Match the expressions below to the type of support, 1 – 8, listed above.

A.   *We had said the end of April for the draft documentation to be out. How realistic is this now in the light of recent holdups?*

B.   *So, Emma, how do you feel it's going?*

C.   *I'd like to revisit some of our earlier decisions.*

D.   *Please email me whenever you want to bounce an idea off someone. You've also got the email addresses and phone numbers of all the people involved in the project – so don't hesitate to use them.*

E.   *I'd like to sit down and talk through how we're going to overcome this particular problem.*

F.   *Are you absolutely sure you've got everything you need?*

G.   *I'll put all this down in black and white to make sure you're quite clear as to the task and your responsibilities.*

H.   *Thank you, that's a job well done as we can see from the very successful outcome.*

The process of delegation

Plan well in advance
⇓
Identify the skill or knowledge needed
⇓
Choose the person for the task
⇓
Explain the task and give clear instructions
⇓
Give authority
⇓
Provide support/feedback

Organising a conference

■ Task 5

Imagine you have to organise a conference. Put the following stages into a logical order by writing the numbers 1 to 12 next to the stages. There may be more than one way of ordering these stages, so don't worry if your suggestion is not exactly the same as the one in the answer key. The first one has been done as an example.

	Decide on promotion
	Order flowers
	Run through the day and check all details
	Calculate an effective budget
	Order catering
	Define layout and seating of venue
	Develop the programme
	Contingency plans for bad weather/latecomers etc.
	Order conference material/presentation kits
1	Define the aims and target audience
	List equipment needed
	Select date and venue

Linking words and phrases/Describing a process

When we describe a simple process, whether it is how to delegate successfully within an office or how a factory produces, for example, paper cups, we usually need to connect our ideas using linking words for sequencing and adding steps. However, when a process or system is more complicated, we may also need to use linkers of reason, purpose, and result, depending on how much detail we have to go into.

There is a summary of linking words and phrases in Appendix A, page 157.

■ Task 6

You are going to email a colleague who is developing the programme for a conference. You would like to make the following points as a result of your experience of the last conference.

▶ programme should be varied

why? danger times: after lunch – energy at low ebb
result – lack of enthusiasm

solution: move speakers round;
select topics or type of activity carefully;
think about the length of session;

Additional note: housekeeping requirements? water, equipment?
I'll need that information for booking

Study the email below and complete each gap with a suitable linking word or phrase. In addition, say which type of linker you have chosen. Choose from: sequencing, adding, reason, purpose or result. The first one has been done as an example.

1.	as a result	result
2.		
3.		
4.		
5.		
6.		
7.		
8.		
9.		

Dear Sasha

How are you getting on finding speakers and putting together the programme for the conference?

I've just been looking through some feedback from the last conference and (1) *as a result*, I'd like to point out the importance of variation within the programme. This is essential (2) .... deal with what I call dangers times; e.g., after lunch, (3) .... this is when delegates' energy is low and (4) .... enthusiasm is at a low ebb. We need, (5) .... to put speakers in different rooms to energise them and (6) .... be very careful about the topic or type of activity we choose to put in these slots. We could also perhaps reduce the time span of the first session after lunch, (7) .... we might find delegates falling asleep!

(8) ...., we should bear in mind any housekeeping requests, e.g., water and equipment requests, (9) .... we can include these in the booking to the venue.

Best wishes
Tom

■ **Scenario for Task 7**

You have been asked to give an introductory talk to new junior members of staff from your offices around Europe on the subject 'Organising a conference'. You have prepared the following talk and because it's in English you've decided to write it out in full.

Organising a conference

Once the target audience and goals for the conference have been established, you'll then be able to determine your approach to organising the conference. Right from the outset, as soon as you've chosen the venue, get support from the venue staff. They know what resources they have and they do this on a full-time basis.

Budgeting plays a vital role. An effective budget is crucial to the success of the conference. Work out your costs. How much is needed for fixed costs, for example, the venue hire, speakers' fees and so on. Then calculate the amount needed for variable costs, such as additional hotel accommodation, extra delegates' packs etc. Again, check your figures with the venue staff and ask for their input. And always allow a contingency of at least 10% to cover unforeseen expenses.

If the conference is to be attended by delegates from overseas offices or by delegates who are not employees of the company, it needs to be promoted through news releases. The Internet is a good resource. Advertisements in specialist magazines and journals need to be placed well in advance. Mail shots of publicity literature can be sent to likely participants. Although the draft program may include the phrase *speaker to be announced*, it is crucial to secure top quality speakers early to ensure a successful promotion campaign. A central system must be set up to receive and track replies, handle bookings, and act as a communications centre.

Conference material is a very important supportive tool. Develop a central theme – a conference identity, much the same as a corporate identity, and use the layout or coloured paper for all communications, for example, name tags, registration cards, note paper, brochures, etc. Delegates will need to be provided with presentation kits with all the relevant documentation: programmes, talk summaries, notepads, handouts, and promotional items as giveaways. Decide what the kits should contain and get these ready for distribution at the conference.

All practical arrangements, for example, the layout and seating at the venue, provision of equipment, and catering can be discussed with the venue staff. As the conference date approaches, a detailed run-through of the day is essential. Make a checklist that you can refer to on the day to make sure that nothing has been overlooked, for example, flowers. These can either create a wonderful atmosphere or make your conference venue look more like a funeral parlour!

Speaking in chunks of meaning

When speaking, whether it is a talk at a conference, a presentation at an in-house meeting or giving instructions to juniors, how we speak can make a huge difference to the listener's ability to 'hear' what you are saying. One important technique is to make sure that you group words into 'sense groups', i.e., divide sentences into parts so that each part carries a 'chunk' of meaning. We usually pause slightly between these parts. Punctuation signals how text can be divided up but very often sentences can be further divided. For example, the first paragraph of the talk above may be divided up as indicated by the slash marks. Of course, there is not only one right way of dividing up speech.

Once the target audience/ and goals for the conference/ have been established,/ you'll then be able/ to determine your approach/ to organising the conference./ Right from the outset,/ as soon as you've chosen the venue,/ get support from the venue staff./ They know what resources they have/ and they do this on a full-time basis./

When we are nervous or feeling under pressure, it's particularly important to be able to control our breathing, allowing plenty of pauses to breathe as we speak. The result is a fluent and confident-sounding speaker who engages the listeners.

■ Task 7

Insert slashes in the rest of the talk on page 48 to indicate chunks of meaning.

Highlighting important words

When we speak, we usually stress or highlight the words which carry important meaning. For example, in the first paragraph of the talk, the underlined words would probably be stressed.

Once the <u>target audience</u>/ and <u>goals</u> for the conference/ have been established,/ you'll then be able to <u>determine</u> your approach/ to organising the conference./ <u>Right</u> from the outset,/ as <u>soon</u> as you've chosen the <u>venue</u>,/ get <u>support</u> from the venue staff./ <u>They</u> know what <u>resources</u> they have/ and they <u>do</u> this on a <u>full-time</u> basis./

■ Task 8

Now underline words which you would stress in paragraph 2.

Budgeting plays a vital role. An effective budget is crucial to the success of the conference. Work out your costs. How much is needed for fixed costs, for example, the venue hire, speakers fees and so on. Then calculate the amount needed for variable costs such as additional hotel accommodation, extra delegates' packs etc. Again, check your figures with the venue staff and ask for their input. And always allow a contingency of at least 10% to cover unforeseen expenses.

5 Complaints

How you complain can make all the difference between resolving a problem quickly and efficiently and severing a business relationship forever. When problems arise, a telephone call may often be the first option in an attempt to put matters right. Make sure every word counts and that it moves the situation on to a satisfactory conclusion.

Complaining by telephone

The scenario

Imagine you've organised for your company to take part in an international trade fair; it's a prestigious event for your company – all the movers and shapers will be there. You have liaised with the trade fair organisers and made all the arrangements: the space required for the stand, the location of the stand, and a small meeting room for more detailed talks with potential clients. However, just two days before the event, you receive a plan of the exhibition hall by post and see that your stand is tucked away in a corner where few people will pass by. You had specifically requested a prominent position near the main entrance. As time is short, you decide to phone the organisers to complain. You are painfully aware that you must do everything you can to secure a better position for your stand. You want to make your point forcefully yet resolve the situation to your satisfaction.

■ Task 1

Match the strategies for complaining in the table to the PA's sentences in the phone call below. The PA's sentences are numbered so that is it easier to complete the table. The PA's part 1 does not match any of the strategies as it's just the introduction to the phone call.

The strategies are in a jumbled order here. The first one has been done as an example.

Strategy for complaining	Number of secretary's part in the phone call
A. Imply that you've understood the solution has been agreed to.	8
B. Indirectly blame but then suggest change is still possible.	
C. Thank and reinforce confirmation of change.	
D. Guarantee change.	

Strategy for complaining	Number of secretary's part in the phone call
E. Propose solution and appeal for help again.	
F. Appeal for help.	
G. Acknowledge other's opinion before stating own.	
H. Play your final card – your compromise.	
I. Sympathise.	

The phone call

PA: 1   This is Susanna Krueger here from Elektra and I'm phoning about the arrangements for the trade fair in London starting on Thursday this week.

Organiser: Ah yes, Susanna, I think all the arrangements are in place, aren't they?

PA: 2   Well, actually, that's what I'm phoning about. I wonder if you could help me with something. I've just received a plan of the exhibition hall and see that our stand has been allocated space in one of the back corners but when I made the arrangements, I requested space near the entrance.

Organiser: Just let me have a look at my plan here ... Ah, yes, you're stand H4. You see, what we have to do is balance the sizes of stands required with the size and shape of the hall. It's quite a juggling feat, I can tell you.

PA: 3   Yes, I can appreciate that but I'd really like our position to be changed.

Organiser: Well, that's rather awkward as the plan's already gone out to all the other exhibitors. And the position you've got is fine. People always seem to walk round in an anti-clockwise direction so they'll soon come across your stand. In fact, it's better than being to the right of the door.

PA: 4   That's interesting, but we've always found being near the door gets us maximum exposure and that's why when I booked the space I specifically requested that area. Have you got my original booking there?

Organiser: Let me look. Yes, you did mention that, but we never make firm promises because as I said before, we have to look at the overall plan and fit everyone in as best we can.

PA: 5   Oh, I took your letter of confirmation of our booking to mean that our requests could be met. If I'd known this was going to be a problem, I could have got back to you and talked about the size of the stand so that we could guarantee our preferred spot. In fact, can't we do that now? We've still got a couple of days.

Organiser: But as I told you, all the exhibitors have been informed of their positions. It's too late to start making changes now.

PA: 6	*Looking at the plan, there does seem to be some space to the right of the door. Couldn't the existing stands be moved along just a metre or so towards our corner, and then we could have our stand there by the door. I really would appreciate your help with this.*
Organiser:	*Well, I don't think that would give you much space.*
PA: 7	*Well, we could always get away with a slightly smaller stand if absolutely necessary. You see, I'll be able to compromise on that if you can get us that position.*
Organiser:	*Well, that might help ...*
PA: 8	*Oh, thank you. That's the solution then, isn't it?*
Organiser:	*Well, I'll do my best. I'd like to talk it through with a colleague first.*
PA: 9	*Good, when will you be able to get back to me to confirm?*
Organiser:	*Certainly before lunch time today.*
PA: 10	*Thank you so much. I knew we'd be able to work something out. Bye.*

Key factors in complaining whilst maintaining the relationship

▶ Wait until your anger or frustration has died down before you phone.

▶ Smile if you're speaking on the telephone, even when complaining, it makes you sound 'human'.

▶ Consider threats or accusations a sign of a breakdown in cooperation. Avoid them if at all possible.

▶ Use words and phrases with positive connotations. e.g., good, certainly.

▶ Always look for solutions and be prepared to compromise.

▶ Be aware of the culture of the person you are talking to. In some cultures it's hard for people to back down; they lose face, so you have to offer an acceptable way out.

▶ Analyse the lead-up to the situation and try to identify what went wrong and when so that it may be possible to avoid it in the future.

▶ Aim to be someone people enjoy doing business with.

Look at these sentences and notice the word order and grammatical structure.

▶ I wonder if you could help me with something.
▶ I'd really like our position to be changed.
▶ Can't we do that?

▷ Couldn't the existing stands be moved?
▷ I really would appreciate your help.
▷ I'd appreciate it if you would look into the matter.

■ Task 2   Sentence structure

Match the beginnings and endings to make complete sentences. Numbers 1, 4 and 6 have two possible endings.

Beginning of sentence	Ending of sentence
1. Couldn't	A. ask for an extension to the deadline?
2. I'd appreciate it if	B. Renate could advise us on this.
3. Can't we	C. the programme be altered?
4. I wonder if	D. your input here.
5. I really would appreciate	E. our reception area to be redesigned.
6. I'd really like	F. you would mention this to Mr. Cox.

■ Task 3   Vocabulary

Read the article below and find words or phrases which mean:

1. complaining
2. getting rid of their shyness
3. clever and well-informed
4. refuse to change their opinion
5. caused
6. quick, without thinking
7. not having confidence
8. careful because you think something may be harmful
9. not showing emotion or complaining
10. making something increase or become stronger
11. criticise
12. no hope for the future

Whingers or discerning customers?

Australians have for years referred to the British as whinging poms; British people emigrated to Australia and then proceeded to complain about everything once they got there! However, many other countries perceive the British as cold and reserved. In fact, there is the phrase 'keeping a stiff upper lip' which means that no matter what is happening, you must maintain your dignity, show no emotion on your face, and remain calm. And this was what every British child was brought up to believe was the right thing to do.

Well, it now seems that the British are shedding their reserve and especially on the consumer front are turning into rather sussed shoppers. They stand their ground, demand their rights and let everyone know about it according to recent statistics. Could it be that now Britain is part of Europe, we have become more hot-blooded? Or was it the turn of the millennium that sparked such a rash change in behaviour? Statistics show that in 2001, more than half of people said they complain all or most of the time if they are unhappy with a product. That was an increase of 12% over the year 2000. Added to that, people believe they are better at it than before.

Interestingly, this may all be the result of becoming an increasingly older nation. According to the national Complaints Culture Survey 2001, it is the older and more experienced members of society who complain the most and the best! Youth and inexperience makes us timid it would seem, in this respect at least. So, be wary of those older, wiser customers and clients – they know what's what. There are surprising regional differences too. The north of England, where traditionally people have been regarded as rather stoical, is the place where people complain the most with nearly two out of three people saying they complain regularly whereas in Wales only one in three people complain.

Could it be that technology is fuelling the complaints culture? Many companies now offer customer service through their website. The turn of the millennium saw a 350% increase in complaints expressed in this way.

What does this mean for companies? Survey findings show that nearly all customers would recommend a company if they had had a complaint which had been resolved efficiently. Of course, the converse is true too. Customers who felt a complaint had been handled badly would badmouth that company to friends, colleagues, and website complaints sites. A bad reputation can spread like wildfire. But in fact, it is not all doom and gloom. When companies learn to take complaints seriously, they can turn a complaint into a positive. Not only can it lead to a stronger relationship with the client but it can also be a learning experience. The client will often say, Why didn't you ... or I'd prefer ... These are times to listen because it is not often that a company gets a free consultancy service!

Letters of complaint

■ Task 4   Letter layout

Match the features of the letter, A – I, to the parts of the letter. The first one has been done as an example.

A. signature	8	1. Weinstrasse 76 67423 Munich
B. addressee		2. 27 August 20XX
C. date		3. Mrs J Stewart Simpsons Constuction Shaftesbury Road London EC5 8JN
D. printed name of the writer of the letter		4. Invoice No. CM 9472
E. body of the letter		5. Dear Mrs Stewart
F. sender's address		6. I am writing concerning our invoice CM 9472 for £2,548.00, a copy of which is enclosed.
G. opening salutation		7. Yours sincerely
H. subject line		8. *M Lemos*
I. closing salutation		9. Mr M Lemos

Opening and closing salutations

The table below outlines the conventions for opening and closing salutations in formal correspondence in British English. In less formal English, for example, when writing to someone you know quite well, the closing salutation may be Kind regards, Best wishes or With very best wishes.

You may find differences in American English and other varieties of English, especially in the form of the closing salutation. In American English the less formal, Yours truly, or Truly yours, are common.

Opening salutation	Status	Closing salutation UK English
Dear Mr X	Married or unmarried male	Yours sincerely
Dear *Mrs X	married female	Yours sincerely
Dear Ms X	Married or unmarried female	Yours sincerely
Dear Sir	Male, name unknown	Yours faithfully
Dear Madam	Female, name unknown	Yours faithfully
Dear Sir/Madam	Name and gender unknown	Yours faithfully

* You should only use Mrs if you know a woman is married and you know they use their married name.

■ Task 5 Punctuation

Read the letter of complaint below and insert punctuation and capitalise letters where appropriate. The first line of the address has been done for you as an example. Do not forget that modern correspondence uses minimal punctuation. If you would like to have an overview of punctuation, turn to Appendix B, page 158.

Mr R Carey
unit 7 travis industrial estate
bolton
bC2 5ge

14 july 20XX

dear mr carey

order no. ty 9642

we are writing with reference to the above order and our letter of june 28 in which we requested information about the delivery of the wallpaper the original agreed delivery date of july 1st has passed and we have been trying to contact you by phone and email but have either not been able to get through to someone who knows about this order or there has been no reply

unless the wallpaper arrives within the next week the completion of one of our jobs will be delayed and we will incur penalty charges we would like to make it clear that we are holding you to your delivery contract and that if we incur penalty charges because of late delivery we will pass these charges on to you

yours sincerely

mr b aksoy
director

■ Task 6 Prepositions

Read through the reply to the letter of complaint above and fill in the gaps with prepositions. The first gap has been completed for you as an example.

15 July 20XX

Dear Mr Askoy,

Thank you (1) for your letter (2) ...... 14th July concerning your order No. TY9642 which was due to be delivered (3) ...... you (4) ...... 28 June.

First, let me apologise (5) ...... the delay (6) ...... getting the wallpaper (7) ...... you and the difficulties you have experienced getting 8 ...... touch (9) ...... us. This was as a result (10) ...... certain main areas (11) ...... our factory being sealed (12) ...... because asbestos was discovered when some refurbishment was being carried (13) .... As you know, health and safety regulations surrounding the presence (14) ...... asbestos are very strict and our hands were tied.

However, I am happy to report that we are now back (15) ...... normal production and your order will be dispatched this Friday, 17 July.

Once again, let me say how much I regret the inconvenience this delay has caused and emphasise that it was due (16) ...... factors (17) ...... our control.

I look forward (18) ...... doing business (19) ...... you again (20) ...... the future and hope that this incident will not adversely affect our relationship.

Yours sincerely

Mr R Carey
Managing Director

Linking words and phrases for comparing and contrasting

When complaining we often need linking words and phrases to compare or contrast situations, for example, from the letter above, *However, I am happy to report ...* . Below are some common linking words for comparing and contrasting. Those separated with a slash have the same meaning. For a comprehensive list of linking words and phrases, refer to Appendix A, page 157.

■ **Task 7**

> in comparison with, (on the one hand) ..... (but) on the other hand, however, in spite of/despite, while/whereas, though/although

Use one of the linking words above to complete each sentence.

1. .... *our best efforts, we have been unable to resolve our difference.*

2. .... *with Drake's estimate, IDF's is quite reasonable.*

3. .... *Stockholm would make a good conference venue .... it would work out rather expensive.*

4. *I have not been able to book you on the 9.15 KLM flight. .... , there is a 10am flight with British Airways.*

5. .... *Larissa has good qualifications, she lacks experience.*

6. *I'm sure Jack's made a good job of the contract. I'd rather check it through myself .... , just to be sure we haven't overlooked anything.*

7. *Which hotel do you think would be most suitable? The Jasper has fantastic facilities .... the Globe is located right in the city centre.*

6 Proposals and reports

There are many similarities between writing a proposal and writing a report. Both require the use of formal language, clear structuring to guide the reader, and careful revision. In this chapter, proposals are dealt with first and then reports.

Proposals

Businesses can fail or thrive depending on how they communicate their ideas and a cleverly developed business proposal can make all the difference.

The term proposal can refer to a wide range of documents, from a bid for a contract to a proposal to increase the budget for the office coffee. Proposals that are seeking funding or an alliance can involve millions of Euros whereas a proposal to give a temporary worker a permanent position has limited financial consequences. No matter what it is, the proposal must make a favourable impression and explain all aspects of the proposed concept clearly and quickly.

First and Foremost/The concept

When you have received the information for a proposal from someone else, i.e., you are not the original author of the proposal, it is imperative that you are clear as to what the concept is. Start off by summarising the concept in 2 or 3 sentences and then show it to a lay person. If they are not absolutely sure what the concept is, rewrite it until they are. Doing this, even when you are the original author, helps clarify the message you want to get across.

■ Task 1

Your own proposal:

You want to propose to the HR department in your company that a full-time permanent post be created in the Accounts Department. A permanent employee did not return from maternity leave and she has not been replaced. At the moment when a crisis occurs, for example, salaries are in danger of not being paid on time and agency staff are brought in at considerable expense. You believe that a person in a permanent post would save money in the long run and allow the Accounts Department to operate under less stressful conditions.

Write a brief outline of your proposal. You may like to use the following headings to guide you.

▶ The problem
▶ The goals
▶ The solution

Know the target reader

Even if your proposal is an internal document, think carefully about who will read it. A proposal is written for the readers not for the writer. When you write a proposal in English, you'll need to know the readers' competence in the English language. Writing for a global audience means avoiding local assumptions and using neutral language rather than overly formal or, conversely, idiomatic phrases. Similarly, find out how conversant the readers are with the jargon of your business or the abbreviations that you use in your line of work. There's nothing worse than ploughing through someone else's gobbledygook.

■ Task 2

A local college is seeking funding from businesses and it has sent you their proposal. Underline the words, terms, and abbreviations in the text below which you think could be clarified or better written in another way. However, don't underline text in brackets at the end as this will be explained later in the proposal.

Vision and rationale

Why X College is seeking funding from the business sector

Local, regional, & national activity points to the need for formal ITT/EPD training for teachers of Business Studies. No national strategy exists to provide them with rigorous professional learning or pedagogy. Training is ad hoc & reliant on collaborative networks which may be limited in sustainability. Funding will provide key teachers with time and resources to experiment & share best/innovative practice much more widely. Ours is not a passive outreach model: it is vital that others are empowered to lead e.g., in targets (mentor cross moderation) 1.3 & 2.4 (peer training by primary mentors in year 4).

■ Task 3

What would you do to deal with the lack of clarity you have underlined?

Let's get writing

Assuming that you understand the concept(s) of the proposal, you've collected and collated all the relevant information and you know your target readers, it's time to get writing. The aim here is to provide language frameworks that can be adapted to suit your particular situation.

Title Page

Begin with a title page or heading that includes the name of the proposal recipient, the title of the project or subject, the name of the author, your company name and address, the date, and, if appropriate, your copyright symbol. How much information you include on the title page or in the heading will very much depend on the status of the proposal and the recipient. You could put a header like this onto appropriate company stationery:

To: . . . .

From: . . . .

Proposal re: . . . .

Date: . . . .

Introductory paragraph

The introductory paragraph should state clearly the purpose of the proposal, e.g.,

▶ *The purpose/aim/intention of this proposal is to ...*

The verb which follows this introductory phrase will vary according to the context, but it might well be one of the following:

▶ *examine/assess/evaluate*
▶ *outline/present/discuss*

e.g.,

The purpose of this proposal is to evaluate the advisability of redesigning the reception area on the ground floor of the Tennison Building.

Alternative openings:

▶ *As requested, this is a proposal concerning/regarding the matter/subject of ...*
▶ *This report outlines the advantages and disadvantages of ...*
▶ *This report contains an assessment of ... which you requested.*

The main body of the proposal

The number and division of paragraphs in the main body of a proposal will obviously depend on the nature of the topic. However, it's always useful when a proposal has clear sub-headings that act as signs to guide the reader through the content. Equally important is the use of linking words to signal:

- the importance of a point, e.g., most importantly, interestingly, significantly
- the addition of information/points
- contrast

(See Appendix A, page 157, for further information on linking words)

The conclusion

To end a proposal, it is usually the case that there is a summary of the main points or argument, followed by a recommendation.

Summarising

To sum up/To conclude/In conclusion/On balance

On the basis of the points mentioned above, it would seem that ...

The only/obvious conclusion to be drawn from these facts is that ...

For the above-mentioned reasons ...

Recommending

It is, therefore, felt/believed/apparent that ... would be suitable/ideal for ...

It would (not) be advisable/advantageous/practical/wise to ...

My/Our recommendation is that ... should be ...

It would appear that ... is/would be the best course of action to take.

■ **Task 4**

The following phrases are too informal for a business proposal. Rewrite them in more formal English.

1. What I want to do in this proposal is ...
2. I want to talk about the positive and negative sides to this.
3. What's really interesting is ...
4. Because of what I said before ...

The language

■ **Task 5**

In addition to the points above regarding suitable phrases and linkers to use, read through the list below and tick which language features you would expect to see in a business proposal.

1. *contractions, e.g., 'we'll' instead of 'we will'*

2. *passive forms, e.g., 'it has been decided' instead of 'we have decided'*

3. *colloquial English, e.g., 'we will get our hands on the money at the end of the month' instead of 'payment will be received at the end of the month'*

4. *ellipsis, e.g., 'Awaiting quotations' instead of 'We are awaiting quotations'.*

5. *long complicated sentences*

And finally

Depending on the extent of your proposal, you may also need to add:

▶   a bibliography, the names and qualifications of the proposal writers or project implementers

▶   a budget which itemises the expenses which would be incurred should the proposal be implemented

▶   materials, equipment, facilities, and personnel required to fulfill the proposal

▶   Appendices

Revision of first draft

When you've written the first draft, take a break so you can distance yourself from what you've written. Then look at it again objectively and ask yourself:

▶ Is the writing clear?

▶ Do the ideas make sense?

▶ Does the layout help the reader focus on the main points?

▶ Have the requirements been fulfilled?

▶ Are the grammar and spelling correct?

▶ How does it sound when read aloud?

▶ What sort of impression will it leave on the reader?

If possible, show your first draft to a colleague who can be trusted to give you constructive feedback on it. Then write the final proposal.

■ Task 6

A colleague of yours has underlined parts of this text that she is unhappy with. It's the summary of a survey to determine consumer awareness of a product. Suggest improvements/corrections for the underlined words or phrases.

For *the basis of the* what we found *above, it would seem that although the quality and* shop *prices of X products are competitive, a* big *percentage of consumers* don't know about *the product range. Furthermore, many of* them *who are aware of the range do not* find the packaging nice enough *to* compel *them to purchase any of the products. Our* idea*, therefore, is that your company* put on *a new advertising* programme *to increase* consumer awareness, to add *to altering the packaging of* all the *range so as to make the products more* attracting *to consumers.*

Reports

As much of the information and langauge for writing proposals is equally relevant to writing reports, this section is made up of short tasks amd checklists which can be used for quick reference.

The purpose of a business report is to convey information to assist in decision-making. The report is the vehicle in which to present this information. Some reports might present the actual solution to a business problem; other reports might record historical information that will be useful to assist future decision-making.

Purpose sentence

The purpose of the report is typically expressed as a statement or a question, e.g.,

▶ To determine ways to reduce waste of office materials.
▶ Should the office be relocated to the main Administration Building?

If you compose the purpose sentence with care, it will ensure that the focus and scope of the report are clear in your own mind.

Creating the report

■ Task 7

Reorganise these steps in the creation of a report into a logical order:

A.   *Analyse the information*
B.   *Determine the solution*
C.   *Determine the scope of the report*
D.   *Gather the information*
E.   *Organise the report*
F.   *Consider the reader(s)*

The reader(s)

In order to clarify who the intended reader(s) of the report are, you might like to use a checklist.

■ Task 8

Study this checklist and add two points which you consider to be important.

▶ *what the reader needs to know from the report*
▶ *educational level*
▶ *knowledge of topic of report*
▶ *responsibility to act*
▶ *age*
▶ *preferences*
▶ *attitudes*
▶ *...*
▶ *...*

Collecting information

Information gathered can be of two types: primary and secondary. Primary is information you collected and recorded yourself. Secondary is collected and recorded by others; it's secondhand.

■ Task 9

Put the sources of information into the appropriate column.

questionnaires, pamphlets, experiments, journals, surveys, newsapers, books, Internet, observations, reports, raw data, magazines.

Primary information	Secondary information

Warning

Both types of information should be used with caution because:
Primary information could be inaccurate or biased.
Secondary information could be inaccurate, biased, and out-of-date.

Analyse the information

The purpose of analysing the information is to make sense, objecively, out of the information you have collected. You must first ensure that the information is free from any personal bias.

Information is then compared and contrasted in order to find new ideas or the best ideas. Separate facts and figures need to be interpreted by explaining what they mean and what significance they have.

Determine the solution

First make sure that a solution is requested. This may not always be the case. The purpose of the report may be to present the facts for someone else to determine the best solution.

If you have been asked to provide a solution, you should be able to do so based on an anlysis of the information.

Organising the report

You're now at the last step of creating a report which was identified in Task 7. Before actually writing the report, work on an outline plan. In order to do this, note down the major ideas, supporting ideas, and details. Then eliminate the irrelevant material you've collected. You'll then have a basic structure for the report.

■ Task 10

Imagine you have been asked to write a report by the Head of Training. He would like you to find out training needs and available courses. Make notes in the skeleton outline below.

To: ....

From: ....

Date: ....

Subject: ....

Purpose of the report ....

Background ....

Supporting data ....

Conclusions and recommendations ....

Writing a rough draft

Don't be too worried about editing and proofreading at this stage. What's important is to start writing. If possible write the report in a logical order. You may, however, prefer to start with the main body of the report but if you do this, be careful not to lose sight of the purpose of the report. Make sure your headings are useful signposts for the reader.

Final report

Check that your report is:

▶ accurate – both in facts and language
▶ objective
▶ clear
▶ concise
▶ readable – i.e., it is easy to read because of the points above

7 Meetings

How often do you hear people complaining about the number of meetings they have to attend and what a waste of time the majority are? And how often do you go to a meeting with no clear idea of what the meeting is hoping to achieve? In fact, many managers who participate regularly in meetings say that most are ineffective. A recent survey by The American Society for Training and Development found that 75% of managers were clearly bothered by the ineffectiveness of typical meetings they attend. Some of their reasons are summarised below.

Ineffective meetings

■ Task 1

Which, in your own experience, are the major characteristics of ineffectiveness? Circle the number which corresponds to the degree to which they bother you.

Characteristic problems at meetings	Not a problem <						> serious
Deviating from the main subject	0	1	2	3	4	5	6
Poor preparation	0	1	2	3	4	5	6
Questionable effectiveness	0	1	2	3	4	5	6
Lack of listening	0	1	2	3	4	5	6
Some participants talk too much	0	1	2	3	4	5	6
Length	0	1	2	3	4	5	6
Lack of participation	0	1	2	3	4	5	6
_____ (?)	0	1	2	3	4	5	6

■ Task 2

In your opinion, what causes these characteristics of ineffectiveness?

How to make meetings more effective

A lot of meetings are called and run on the basis that everyone knows what the goal of a meeting is – don't assume that this is always the case or that all participants share a common purpose. However, there are things you can do to make meetings more effective:

▶ have a clear agenda
▶ elect a focused chairperson
▶ ask someone to write the minutes

The agenda

All agendas should list the following:

▶ title of meeting
▶ date
▶ start time
▶ end time
▶ location
▶ topics to be discussed

and should be accompanied by the relevant background information.

■ Task 3

You are based in London. Your company has grown in size over the last few years and is, therefore, opening a second office not too far away from the present one. The Sales & Marketing Departments will be relocated to the new office. You are the PA to the CEO and have been asked to chair a meeting for all support staff to inform them of the move and to answer any questions. The meeting will last for 2 hours and will take place in Meeting Room 1. Write the agenda.

Chairing a Meeting

■ Task 4

Find words in the text which mean:

1. general agreement by a group
2. a person who assists in the birth of a baby
3. stepping in
4. range
5. assigned
6. express something in a different way to make it easier to understand
7. accept as a compromise

A facilitator/chairperson is someone who helps a group of people understand their common objectives and plan to achieve them without personally taking any side of the argument. The facilitator will try to assist the group in achieving consensus. The role has been compared with that of a midwife who assists in the process of creation but is not the producer of the end result.

The basic skills of a facilitator are about following good meeting practices: timekeeping, following an agreed-upon agenda, and keeping a clear record. The higher-order skills involve watching the group, its individuals, and their process, and knowing the art of intervening in a way that adds to the group's creativity rather than taking away from it.

Some of the things facilitators do to assist a meeting:

▶ clarify the purpose, scope, and deliverables of the meeting or workshop

▶ keep the group on track to achieve its goals in the time allotted

▶ either provide the group or help the group decide what ground rules it should follow and remind them of these when they are not followed

▶ guide the group through processes designed to help them listen to each other and create solutions together

▶ ask open-ended questions that stimulate thinking

▶ paraphrase and summarize contributions to confirm understanding and ensure they are heard by the whole group

▶ ensure the group doesn't settle for the first thing that they can agree on because they find it painful to go on disagreeing with each other

▶ offer opportunities for quieter members to participate

▶ ensure that actions and next steps are agreed on by the group
(adapted from Wikipedia)

■ Task 5

What should a facilitator not do? For example:

▶ *dominate the meeting*
▶
▶
▶

■ Task 6

Match the expressions 1 – 16 to the tasks a) – j) that an effective chairperson/ facilitator would do. There may be more than one expression for a task. Write the letter of the task in the box. The first one has been done for you.

Expressions	Tasks
1. So, Alice agreed to ..., can we have your response by next week?	*j*
2. What do you think of ...?	
3. Will a coffee break at 11 be OK?	
4. I'd like to thank everyone for coming and ...	
5. Can I just summarise the main points/views/problems?	
6. Can we come to your point later, please?	
7. May I suggest we begin by ...?	
8. Great, could you outline the problem as you see it?	
9. So, what you're saying is ...	
10. OK, I suggest we finish. We've achieved our main objectives.	
11. Can we all agree on this? Good, well let's move on ...	
12. Now, as you probably know ...	
13. Right, as we've agreed in principle to ... the only thing left is to ...	
14. Mrs XYZ will take notes ... you'll all get a copy later	
15. Just a minute Corinna, let Martina finish what she's saying	
16. If I understand you correctly, you mean ...	

Tasks
a)   Getting people's attention and opening the meeting
b)   Giving the background to the meeting
c)   Agreeing the general process
d)   Suggesting procedures
e)   Assigning roles
f)   Ensuring clarity from the participants for the benefit of everyone
g)   Keeping the discussion moving forward
h)   Keeping control
i)   Securing agreement
j)   Closing the meeting/summing up/next steps

Participating in a meeting

Very often, of course, we don't chair a meeting, we are participants and have to express ourselves in a way that doesn't offend anyone but yet allows us to convey our message clearly.

■ Task 7

Underline and number the expressions in the following dialogue that:

1. express agreement
2. express disagreement
3. make suggestions
4. interrupt
5. deal with interruptions

Christine: *I think the move is a bad idea because if sales and marketing are in a different place, ...*

Helene: *No hang on a minute ... you know we're really overcrowded here and ...*

Christine: *Let me finish what I'm saying please ... what I wanted to say is that it'll take longer to get, say, a particular piece of information if we're physically in different buildings and if ...*

Helene: *I don't think so ... we'll just use the phone and email more and it'll save time*

Christine: *Yeah, OK I guess you're right there but what about face-to-face meetings – those'll just get harder and ...*

Helene: *Yes but why don't we schedule them in? It'll be more time-effective than just seeing each other on an ad-hoc basis.*

Expressions for agreeing/disagreeing and giving opinions

Here are some other expressions you can use to express agreement/disagreement, depending on how strongly you feel.

Agreement – strong	I completely agree/I'm in total agreement
Agreement – neutral	I agree/I think I can accept your position on that
Agreement – partial	I agree in principle but .../I I take your point but have you thought about ...
Disagreement – strong	You're completely mistaken/Under no circumstances could I agree to that

Disagreement – neutral	I disagree/I can't go along with that
Softening disagreement	I'm sorry but .../I respect your point of view, however ...

Giving opinions

Another thing we usually have to do in meetings is to express our opinions and/or ask others for theirs. Here are some expressions you can use to do this:

Giving opinions – strong	I'm absolutely convinced that .../There's no doubt in my mind that ...
Giving opinions – neutral	As far as I'm concerned/From my point of view
Giving opinions – tentative	It seems to me that .../I would say that ...
Asking for opinions – to one person	What's your position on this, Ms X?/I'd be interested to hear your views on this, Mr Y
Asking for opinions – to a group	What's the general feeling about this?/Does anyone have any comments to make?

■ Task 8

Your entire building is going to be non-smoking. You have been asked for your opinion on the proposed change at a meeting – express your opinion backed up by your reasons.

Minutes

Generally, after each meeting minutes are distributed to the participants and forwarded to those who were unable to attend. Minutes should be written up and distributed as soon as possible after the meeting to reduce errors of memory. They should be concise and to the point and should not be a transcript of the entire meeting.

■ Task 9

What should be included in the minutes of a meeting? For example:

▶ *date, time, and venue*
▶
▶
▶
▶

Sample Minutes

The regular weekly meeting of the marketing department was held on Friday, August 10, 20XX at 11 a.m. All department members were present. The minutes of the previous month's meeting were read and approved.

The reports from the marketing research institutes have been received and placed on file.

The new marketing strategy was discussed and consensus reached that we should proceed with market research. All participants present agreed that we would go ahead with the X Market Research Institute as they seem to be the most appropriate for our new product. They will carry out a consumer survey on our behalf to determine acceptance of our new product, establish what competitors are currently pricing similar products at, and will come back with recommendations to us on pricing and positioning.

Ms R has agreed to be the contact person for the research institute and will report back on their progress at our next marketing meeting. The next meeting will take place at 11 a.m. on Friday August 17, 20XX.

8 Writing promotional copy

This unit merges all the skills required to produce good promotional copy. Copywriters need a flair for writing this kind of text as well as editing and proofreading skills.

Editing is what you begin doing as soon as you finish your first draft. You scrutinise the content. Moreover, you want to reread it to see, for example, if the text is well-organised, and if the transitions (for example, linking words) between sentences and/ or paragraphs are smooth.

Proofreading is the final stage of the editing process, focusing on surface errors such as misspellings and mistakes in grammar and punctuation. You should proofread only after you have finished all of your other editing revisions.

What's the purpose of the text you're writing?

This may seem a simplistic question but it's one that's easy to ignore when there's the buzz of an advertising drive running through the company. The question should be made more specific: is the aim to advertise your brand or to get a direct response (a purchase or a request for a brochure)?

Two types of advertising

Brand advertising is used by big companies to build and increase awareness of their brand. This type of advertising can consume huge amounts of money and is rarely appropriate for smaller companies.

Direct response advertising is used when you want to get a clear response: a sale or an enquiry.

Understanding the distinction between these two types of advertising will have a huge influence on how you write your copy. However, one thing is always certain; you have to have a catchy headline. The headline is either the heading that goes at the top of the ad or if there's no heading, it's the first words of the ad. If you're on the radio, it's the first thing people hear. If it's TV, it's the first thing they see and hear. The headline needs to grab people's attention.

Getting the reader's attention: Headlines

Headlines have to be intriguing, eye-catching, and clever without being totally obscure. See if you can predict what sort of company ran these headlines.

■ Task 1

Match the advertisement headline to the company.

Headlines

1. On November 17*th* 2006, we set fire to our client's factory. It's all part of the service.

2. *More*
   Business
   Acumen

3. Could a greener fleet boost your company's growth?

4. Find your Shangri-La HERE

5. DIRK RAVENSTEINER, ACCEPTING IMPOSSIBLE MISSIONS DAILY.

6. In keeping with the Touareg's seductive lines, here's another.
   Over £3,000 of extras, for free.

7. Efficiency is the fuel of success

Companies

a.   a business school
b.   a car manufacturer
c.   an insurance company
d.   a courier company
e.   a hotel
f.   a vehicle management company
g.   an airline

The principles of writing promotional copy

There are some techniques that may help you write advertising copy. One useful classic formula used by advertisers is AIDA. This stands for:

Attention
Interest
Desire
Action

Attention – as already mentioned, the headline has to attract the readers' attention.

Interest – and once you've got their attention, you need to create an interest in your product or service.

Desire – you've then got to convert that interest into a strong desire for your product or service.

Action – and then you've got to convert that desire into action. At the end of the ad, you need a call to action. Tell people exactly what they need to do to follow through and make it easy for them to do so. This is where many people go wrong. Even if you have a good ad, you still need to tell people precisely what to do – how to take action.

Look through your company's advertising and see if it follows this advice.

Attention

Remember that this is the crucial starting point. If you don't attract the readers' attention in the first place, then all the other techniques will be worth nothing. When you look at the examples of headlines in Task 1, you'll notice that companies use shock tactics, clever abbreviations, indirect promises of growth, freebies and success, and the appeal of the daring action man all in an attempt to catch the reader's eye.

Interest

Punctuation

In addition to the vocabulary and style of the ad, correct punctuation leads the reader smoothly through the text. It's part of maintaining the interest. If the punctuation is wrong, the reader may get confused and give up.

Checking punctuation is a proofreading task but it has been included here because it also affects the readers' interest.

■ Task 2

Punctuate the following advertisement and include capital letters where necessary.

Can a mere radish drive customer loyalty in a way yes we worked with a major grocer to develop a unique scale that identifies and prices produce through a plastic bag so checkout queues move faster technology innovations like this coupled with business innovations such as *RFID inventory control give this grocer a real competitive edge how did it happen we put together a team of supply chain management specialists systems analysts and engineers who melded vendors variable pricing strategies and visionary (literally) scale want innovation for loyalty talk to the innovators innovator to learn more visit:

* Radio Frequency Identification Technology

Read Appendix B, page 158, for the basic rules of punctuation.

Curiosity

Another sure way to create interest and desire is to arouse the readers' curiosity. One recent ad did this by using new words; words which have scarcely reached any dictionary yet. This ad was run by a magazine. The aim was to get people to want to read a particular survey.

> ## Blogs, vlogs, metaverses, folksonomies, podcasts.
>
> ### Will new media have as big an effect on business, society and politics as they are having on dictionaries?
>
> ### Read the survey on new media.

Your curiosity might well be aroused if you'd never heard these words before, or you'd only vaguely heard of them, but weren't absolutely sure what they mean.

■ Task 3

Put each of these words: blog, vlog, metaverse, folksonomy, podcast, in the gap before its definition.

1. .... : *a word coined by Neal Stephenson's science fiction novel Snow Crash (1992) constitutes Stephenson's vision of how a virtual reality-based Internet might evolve in the near future.*

2. .... : *is a Web-based publication consisting primarily of periodic articles (normally in reverse chronological order).*

3. .... : *is a collaboratively generated, open-ended labeling system that enables Internet users to categorize content such as Web pages, online photographs, and Web links.*

4. .... : *is a blog which uses video as the primary content; the video is linked to a videoblog post and usually accompanied by supporting text, image, and additional metadata to provide context. It has become a significant contributor to clip culture.*

5. .... : *is the method of distributing multimedia files, such as audio programs or music videos, over the Internet for playback on mobile devices and personal computers.*

(Definitions from wikipedia.com)

If you come across new words which aren't in the dictionary, try looking them up on wikipedia.com

Rhetorical questions

You'll notice in the ad on blogs etc. the use of a question. This device is common among advertisers. An airline used it in the headline and body of this ad.

What does £29 buy you these days? Take a seat.

■ Task 4

This is the rest of the copy for the ad above. Complete the gaps with the phrases in the box. Write capital letters as appropriate.

we'd beg to differ / we don't mean / we hope so / all of which / it does

Would you be surprised to learn that a flight to Europe costs from as little as £29 one-way? (1) .... , especially when you consider what's included.

Firstly, our service. You are our guest and should expect to be treated as such.

You should also expect the option to check-in online and to print your own boarding pass on all routes from the UK to Europe. Some think the British are keen on queuing. (2) ....

There's also our network, which currently covers over 300 destinations. And when we say we fly to a destination, (3) .... a small town fifty miles from it.

(4) .... brings us back to the seat itself. With us you're still allocated one.

Essentially, we believe your holiday should start long before you arrive at your destination. With British Airways, (5) ....

Spelling

Once you've got the concept, and carefully chosen the vocabulary and images for your ad, you write your text. You then need to check and recheck.

There are certain cases where you cannot rely on the spellchecker on the computer; the spelling may be correct but it could be the wrong word.

■ Task 5

Correct the spelling in this advertisement. None of these spelling mistakes showed up using a typical spellchecker programme.

As the official shipping and logistical partner for Mission Impossible III, we needed a man like Dirk Ravensteiner on the ground. Dirk and his teem made sure the preps, sets, and high-tech equipment were in places when the cameras reeled. Weather it was in Rome, Shanghai, Berlin or Los Angeles, it was truly an amazing performance. It's the spirit of can do and the experience of know-how. We call it Do How.

Desire

Looking through ads, you'll see that desire is often created by appealing to our basest instincts: competitiveness, envy, greed, and sex, to mention but a few.

TV ads in particular often show how you can not only keep up with the Jones, but you can actually go one better by having a flasher car, whiter washing, and a greener weed-free lawn. Generally speaking, these ads are there to convince us that our aspirations can be realised.

Action

Direct response advertising aims to convert the readers' interest and desire into action, and it's got to be easy for the reader to buy the product or contact the company.

■ Task 6

Write a second call to action similar to the first one.

Example

To find out more, visit www.trendsolutions.com

visit www.trendsolutions.com for more information

1. ordering is easy: call 0500 00 50 30
   Call 0800 325 7989 ....

2. SAVE OVER £108.00 A YEAR
   Always .... prices

3. BUY NOW, GET MORE!
   BUY .... FREE

4. Hurry! special offer ends 26th JULY
   .... days to ....

■ Task 7

There are two mistakes in each of the numbered paragraphs below. They could be spelling, punctuation or grammar mistakes. Find them and correct them. The text is written in American English.

The Proofreading process

Experiment with different tactics until you find a system that works well for you. The important thing is to make the process systematic and focused so that you eliminate as many errors as possible in the least amount of time.

▷ 1. *Don't rely entirely on spellcheckers.* These can be useful tools but they are far from foolproof. Spellcheckers have a limited dictionary, so some words that show up as misspelled may just not be in their memory. In addition spellcheckers will not catch misspellings that from another valid word. For example, if you type "moor" instead of "more", "to" instead of "too", or "there" instead of "their", the spellchecker won't pick up the error.

▷ 2. *Grammar checkers can be even more problematic.* These programs works with a limited number of rules, so they can't identify every error and often make mistakes. They also fail to give thorough explanations to help you understand why a sentence should be revised. You need to be able to evaluate the feedback it provides.

▷ 3. *Proofread for only one kind of error at a time.* If you try to identify and revise to many things at once you risk losing focus and your proofreading will be less effective. It's easier to catch grammar errors if you aren't checking punctuation and spelling at the same time. In addition, some of the techniques that work well for spotting one kind of mistake won't work for others.

▷ 4. *Read slowly and read every word.* Try reading out loud which forces you to say each word and also let's you hear how the words sound together. When you read silently or too quickly, you may skip over errors or make unconscious corrections.

▷ 5. *Separate the text into individual sentences.* This is another technique to help you to read every sentence carefully. Simply press the return key after every full stop so that every line begins a new sentence. Then read each sentence separately, looking for grammer, punctuation, or spelling errors. If you're working with a printed copy, try use an opaque object like a ruler or a piece of paper to isolate the line you're working on.

▷ 6. *Circle every punctuation mark.* This forces you look at each one. As you circle, ask yourself if the punctuation are correct.

▷ 7. *Read the paper backwards.* This technique is helpful for checking spelling. Start with the last word on the last page and work your way back to the begining, reading each word separately. Because content, punctuation, and grammar wont make any sense, your focus will be entirely on the spelling of each word.

▷ 8. *Proofreading is a learning process.* Your not just looking for errors that you recognize; you're also learning to recognize and correct new errors. This is where handbooks and dictionnaries come in. Keep the ones you find helpful close at hand as you proofread.

▷ 9. *Look it up.* You'll often find things that don't seem quite right to you, but you're not quite sure what's wrong neither. A word looks like it might be misspelled, but the spellchecker didn't catch it. You think you need a comma between two words, but you're not sure why. Should you use "that" instead of "which". If you're not sure about something, look it up.

▶ ***10. The proofreading process becomes more efficient as you develope and practice a systematic strategy.** You'll learn to identify the specific areas of your own writing that need carefull attention **and** knowing that you have a sound method for finding errors will help you to focus more on developing your ideas while drafting the text.*

If you get copy back with editor's symbols and you'd like to check what they mean, look at Appendix C, page 161.

■ Task 8

Now put all your copywriting skills together and improve this text. It's a company's vision statement which will appear on their home page on their website.

Group Overview.

VISION

We aim to be the leader in formulation science. We have, and want to build even more a portfolio of businesses, that are big players in their respective big industries bringing together a knowledge of customer wants with recent technology platforms to provide products for our customers. With this attributes we want to make superior value for our customs and shareholders but not compromising our commitment to safety health and the environment and the communities where we work.

9 Apologising

There is a saying in English which goes *Sorry is the hardest word to say*. This is strange because many non-native speakers of English believe the opposite – that it's the easiest word to say because English speakers seem to say it so often in so many different situations! How you use your voice is crucial, as is your choice of language.

Saying sorry

■ **Task 1**

What does *I'm sorry* mean, a. – c. in sentences 1 – 3?

a. I regret ...
b. Excuse me,
c. I beg your pardon.

1. Sorry, I think that's my seat.
2. It's too hot in here now. I'm sorry I asked the building manager to increase the temperature in the offices.
3. Sorry, what did you say?

Sorry or *I'm sorry* can also be used to signal politeness. What is *I'm sorry* used to signal in sentences 4 – 9?

d. disagree
e. refuse permission
f. make a request
g. refuse a request
h. refuse an invitation
i. give bad news

4. Sorry, could you move your car? You're blocking me in.
5. I'm sorry, the repairs are going to be rather expensive.
6. I'm sorry, but I can't go along with you there.
7. I'm sorry, I can't let you have Friday off as we have to ...
8. I'm sorry, you can't take drinks into the laboratory.
9. I'm sorry I won't be able to make it because ...

■ **Task 2**

What would say in the following situations? Use appropriate phrases from Task 1, a, b or c.

1.   *A colleague is using a meeting room that you had booked.*

2.   *You're having difficulty finding a venue for the staff Christmas party. You wish you had booked something earlier.*

3.   *You need to point out to a junior that the book he wants cannot be taken out of the library.*

4.   *You won't be able to go to the pub with the rest of the staff tonight because you've got visitors at home.*

5.   *You did not catch what a colleague said.*

Accepting apologies

When we accept an apology we can accept graciously using phrases such as:

▶   That's OK. No problem. Don't mention it.
▶   It's quite all right. It's not important. Don't worry about it.

When we decide not to accept an apology we can say:

▶   I'm afraid that's not good enough, I'd rather you didn't let it happen again.

A more subtle way of not accepting an apology is to pretend it hasn't been made, for example:

A: I'm sorry I'm late.   B: Well, let's get started, shall we?
A: I'm sorry I lost it.   B: I'll go and get another one.

■ **Task 3**

Respond to the following prompts.

1.   *I'm really sorry the refreshments weren't ready in time for the morning coffee break for your meeting with Richard.*

2.   *Gosh, I seem to be late again, sorry.*

3.   *I'm sorry, they didn't have a chicken sandwich so I've brought you a salad one instead. Hope that's all right?*

Your voice

The key, tone, and pace of our voice are important ways by which we communicate the seriousness or otherwise of our message. They can also make the hearer/listener sympathetic or irritated. Of course, these aspects of speech, and our reactions to them, depend on our culture.

Key

What is key? It is when we raise or drop our voice to a higher or lower level.

What is the effect of key?

Low key

Changing to low key means the information is low key.

▶ It is what the audience would expect. (It confirms their expectations.)
▶ It is an aside. (something you would find in brackets or in inverted commas)

Example

1. It will take a long time to put right, and cost a great deal.
2. ... an increase of one hundred million dollars, three per cent of the total.
3. I'm sorry to say, growth is, in the main, slowing down owing to ...

N.B. Low key is also used to show we have come to the end of a 'verbal paragraph', after which we would begin again in high key.

■ Task 4

Rewrite the following sentences to indicate in which part of the sentence the voice would drop to confirm the audience's expectations. See the three examples above.

1. There are several methods, as outlined before, a company can use when looking to fill staff vacancies.

2. Headhunting is a cost-effective way of hiring staff, and it works.

3. Six applicants were short listed, out of 24.

4. Companies can justify the expense, and we know just how expensive it can be, of going to a headhunter.

High key

Changing to high key occurs when we want to show a word or concept is in contrast with:

▶ something we said before
▶ something we will say in the near future
▶ the implicit expectations of our audience (i.e., something surprising)
▶ we want to show a new 'verbal paragraph'

Example

1. This year we increased our net profit by ^{twenty} million dollars.
2. These results have been encouraging ^{however,} there are problems.
3. ^{Right} then, let's move on to my second topic.

■ Task 5

Rewrite the following sentences to indicate in which part of the sentence the voice would rise to signal high key. See the three examples above.

1. *Only six people have replied to my memo?*
2. *It's true it's going to be difficult, but there is a way we could ...*
3. *I'm sorry, I wanted the figures for March, not February.*
4. *Wasn't it Jane who contacted Mr. Zappala before?*

Dealing with tricky situations

There are times when things go wrong and all we can do is apologise, accept blame when we are at fault, assure the client that this will not happen again, and promise to do something to rectify the situation.

These situations are often stressful for the people involved so how we use our voice is of particular importance. Part of the skill of a good communicator is creating a sense of *we*. This is more effective in getting the listener's support than the creation of an *I-you* relationship. We can strengthen this effect by using the tone of our voice appropriately.

Written apologies

Different forms of the word "apology" are used in more formal situations, e.g.,

▶ Jan Becks sends his apologies for not attending the meeting.
▶ We apologise for the delay in getting the goods to you.
▶ Please accept our apologies for this mistake.

When we think about larger companies, organisations, government departments, and so on, there are said to be two responses to errors.

▶ Members of effective organisations come together and put right whatever is wrong.

▶ Members of ineffective organisations cannot be seen for dust as they scatter to avoid the blame.

■ Task 6

The letter below is from a bank to a property letting agency. The property agency collects rent for premises and the rent goes into the bank. The bank then credits the landlords' accounts.

Read the letter below and answer the following questions

1. Why is the bank having to write a letter of apology?
2. What is the bank promising to do?

Your Ref. BVF/KJ
Our Ref. MNG

Dear Mr X

I am writing formally in response to your letter of the 25th October following our earlier conversations regarding the content. Let me once again apologise to you personally that you have had cause to complain that our service has failed to deliver in the key area of processing your clients' monthly payments, which is clearly essential to the reputation of your business.

The fact is that you had properly instructed us to make the regular monthly payments to your clients to ensure that the credits were placed to their accounts on Wednesday 14th September. In the event, your clients did not receive the credits until Monday 19th September. The delay was caused as a result of our processing issue and should not be taken as any reflection on your integrity or credit rating. We were wholly at fault.

Having discussed this matter with you, I can confirm that if any of your clients who have incurred bank charges, interest charges or penalty charges as a result of this bank processing error can obtain evidence from their banks in confirmation, we will reimburse any of the identified charges directly caused by this payment delay.

I am very sorry that I have to write to you in this way as it reflects a breakdown of the high service standards that I have set locally. Hopefully the actions detailed in this letter and recently discussed will at least alleviate some of the potential consequences of our error.

Yours sincerely

XXXX
Area Manager

■ **Task 7**

Highlight the phrases in the letter used:

1. *to express an apology*
2. *to accept blame*
3. *to reassure the addressee that their financial standing will not be affected*
4. *to promise action*
5. *to express hope that they have to some extent rectified the situation*

■ **Task 8**

In the scenario above where the landlords did not receive payments into their bank accounts on time, the property letting agency had to write and apologise to the landlords. Complete the agency's letter of apology with words/phrases from the box.

> *beyond / in full / made worse / remedy / resulted in / sincere / subject to / unfortunately*

October 14, 20XX

Accounts Office

Some clients will be aware that, (1) ...., during September we had some difficulties in the Accounts Office. Regrettably, a senior member of the Accounts Office was off on long-term sick leave which (2) .... the department being temporarily short staffed. We have taken measures to (3) .... this. The Accounts Office is now being run with assistance by Carol Weston and Andrew Jackson.

The problem was unfortunately (4) .... by a problem with our Internet banking which is the method by which payments are made to clients. This problem took some time for X Bank to resolve and was (5) .... our control. X Bank have acknowledged the problem and if any client was (6) .... interest charges or any other unexpected bank charges as a result of some late payment of monies, these charges will be refunded (7) .... on production of a bank statement or bank letter highlighting them (we need to be able to forward this physical proof to X bank who are underwriting this).

We do not expect any further problems and offer our (8) .... apologies for any difficulties that have arisen as a result of these matters which were out of our hands.

The language of apologies

Apologies					
May I/we I/We would like to I/We	apologise				for ...
May I/we I/We would like to I/We	offer extend	my our	sincere profound	apologies	for
	Please accept	my our	sincere profound	apologies	for
Accepting blame					
I/We	accept			responsibility	for
I/We	accept acknowledge grant			(the fact)	that
This problem	was caused	as a result of	our	system error	
Assurances					
	Please accept	my our	(personal)	assurance guarantee undertaking	that
Let	me us I/We can	(person- ally)	assure guarantee promise reassure	you	that

■ **Task 9**

The scenario:

A good customer ordered 6 boxes of product CJ 784510. The order should have been delivered on 20th June. However, due to problems at the logistics company you use, the delivery is late. Your customer has telephoned to complain. You have looked into the problem and have got a guaranteed date of 4th July for delivery.

Write a letter of apology to your customer. Explain the problem and promise delivery on 4th July. Use expressions from the table above.

10 Giving presentations with impact

Giving a presentation can strike fear into the heart of even the most experienced presenter but careful preparation can contribute a lot to reducing stress levels. Before you begin the preparation phase, it can be helpful to ask yourself the following questions.

Checklist

▶ have you asked yourself what you want from the presentation?
▶ do you want action as a result of your presentation or are you informing?
▶ is it well-prepared?
▶ is it well-rehearsed?
▶ is it the right length?
▶ have you put yourself in the audience's shoes?
▶ are you thinking positively?

Once you've brainstormed the content of your presentation, your thoughts will turn to the visual aids you want to use to support and add interest to the message you want to convey.

Using slides

Slides significantly improve the interest of a presentation but they must obviously be relevant to what you want to say. They should support you, as the speaker, but not become the entire focus of the presentation and overwhelm you and your audience.

■ **Task 1**

Have a look at the 3 slides which follow and analyse what's wrong with them.

Slide 1

Clever Industries Inc.

The Meaning of Banking

► A **bank** [bæŋk] is a business which provides financial services for profit. Traditional **banking services** include receiving deposits of money, lending money and processing transactions. Some banks (called Banks of issue) issue banknotes as legal tender. Many banks offer ancillary financial services to make additional profit; for example: selling insurance products, investment products or stock broking.

► Currently in most jurisdictions the business of banking is regulated and banks require permission to trade. Authorization to trade is granted by bank regulatory authorities and provide rights to conduct the most fundamental banking services such as accepting deposits and making loans. There are also financial institutions that provide banking services without meeting the legal definition of a bank (see banking institutions).

► Banks have a long history, and have influenced economies and politics for centuries.

► Traditionally, a bank generates profits from transaction fees on financial services and from the interest it charges for lending. In recent history, with historically low interest rates limiting banks' ability to earn money by lending deposited funds, much of a bank's income is provided by overdraft fees and riskier investments.

► The name *bank* derives from the Italian word *banco, desk,* used during the Renaissance by Florentines bankers, who used to make their transactions above a desk covered by a green tablecloth.

Slide 2

Slide 3

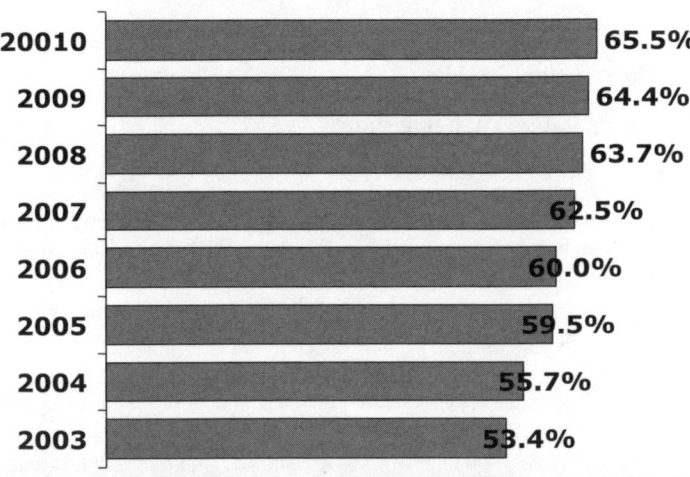

- ■ **Task 2**

a)   How could the slides be improved?
b)   Present the same information so it is easier to read.

> *Poverty rates*
>
> *In region A poverty stands at 11%*
> *Here, in region B poverty is 22%*
> *Region C has 8%*
> *Region D is the highest with 43%*

Here is a list of best-practice points to remember when you're creating and using slides.

Dos

▶ make the point size at least 18

▶ try to limit the number of words you put on a slide to a maximum of 12 – 20 if you can

▶ use only one main idea per slide

▶ have a compelling action title

▶ avoid talking while you're changing slides

▶ don't turn your back to the audience

▶ don't simply read what is on your slide – your audience is literate

■ **Task 3**

What are the don'ts of using slides?

....

....

....

....

....

Action titles of slides

■ **Task 4**

Write a simple, clear, and unambiguous title for slides dealing with these contexts.

1. *People who are aged between 21 – 35 are finding it increasingly difficult to get on the property ladder as house prices have shot up and they are having to find larger and larger deposits which is often very hard for them as they usually don't earn very much.*

2. *A recent survey in the UK demonstrated unequivocally that females in the workplace are generally remunerated to a lower degree than their male counterparts.*

3. *In the past, secretaries were expected to be at the beck and call of their bosses and did everything from buying their wives flowers to taking their suits to the drycleaners; nowadays, however, a secretary can be a project manager, a team leader, a mentor to juniors, as well as the right hand of her boss.*

Ordering a presentation

When giving a presentation, it's tempting to follow a chronological approach starting with e.g., the task, how you approached it, the conclusions you came to, and then your recommendations. Very often it's best to begin with the recommendations arrived at and then spend the rest of the time telling your audience why you think that this is the best answer – especially if you are under a time constraint.

Have a look at this letter from a girl to her 'best' friend.

Dear Anna

Do you remember last Saturday when I went to the cinema with my boyfriend and you happened to be there so you came and sat with us. My boyfriend told me that when I was in the ladies, you kissed him.

Also when you came to lunch with my family on Sunday and my mother cooked a roast dinner, you said that it was the worst Sunday lunch you had ever eaten.

Yesterday when we met in the park as I was walking my dog, he brushed against your leg, and you kicked him and said you would set your Alsatian on him.

Well for all these reasons I really hate you and I don't want to be your friend any more.

Michaela

Source: Adapted from Gene Zelazny: "Say it with Presentations"

■ Task 5

Rewrite the letter above in slide format from the bottom-up – putting the conclusion first, followed by the reasons. You will need to shorten the sentences too.

Structuring a presentation

■ Task 6

Underline and number the phrases which match stages 1 – 6 in the following introduction to a presentation.

1. *Duration*
2. *Introducing topic*
3. *Questions*
4. *Outlining main points*
5. *Introducing self*
6. *Greetings*

Good morning ladies and gentlemen. First of all, I'd like to introduce myself. I'm from Company XYZ and my name's Helga Braun. As you may know, I'm responsible for organizing this Office Congress and I'd like to thank you for giving me the opportunity to talk to you about the two-day program. I'm going to divide my presentation into three main sections: the plenary sessions, the workshops, and the special lectures given by keynote speakers. I plan to speak for about 10 minutes and will be happy to take any questions at the end.

Here are some other expressions you can use to move through and end a presentation.

▶ *Starting your first point*
OK. So let's begin with my first point.

▶ *Finishing a point*
So, to summarize my (first) point ...

▶ *Moving on to a new point*
I'd like to move on to my next point.
This brings me to my next point ...

▶ *Referring back*
I'd like to return (for a moment) to ...

▶ *Handling (unwanted) interruptions*
Can I come back to that later?
Good question. In fact, I'm going to answer that in my next point. OK?

▶ *Referring to visuals*
I'd like to draw your attention to ...
As you can see in this slide ...

▶ *Inviting questions prior to your closing remarks*
If you have any questions, I'll be happy to answer them.

▶ *Summarizing*
Finally, let's review the main points again.
So, just to summarize ...
Firstly, we looked at ...
Secondly, I showed you ...
Finally, I analyzed ...
In the Question and Answer session we discussed ...

▶ *Concluding*
In conclusion ...
I'd like to finish by saying ...
Thank you again for giving me this opportunity to ...

Tips

It is never a good idea to read from a prepared script because it doesn't allow you to interact with the audience and they might just as well have watched you on TV! However, what many presenters do, particularly if they are presenting in a foreign language, is put key words on cards. The thing not to forget is firstly, to number the cards in case you drop them on the floor and secondly, mark on your cards the slide number that goes with them. Alternatively, of course, you could print out an overview of your slides and write key words in the notes section.

■ Task 7

Three teams from your company have been asked to organize an event in London lasting for two days for your company and its foreign subsidiaries. You are representing your team and you are going to present your proposal to your boss and several other managers from your company.

Have a look at the information below, then a) write out the introduction to your presentation in full and b) write brief notes that you would put on cards/slides for the details of the program.

Wednesday: Arrival at Heathrow at 6 o'clock; transfer to Marriott Hotel Knightsbridge; drinks in the bar at eight; dinner in the hotel restaurant at 9. Thursday: welcoming speech by the CEO at nine; presentations by delegates from SE Asia between 9.30 – 11.30; break then for half an hour; then an hour of round-table discussions followed by lunch from 1 – 2 pm in the hotel restaurant again; then two hours of presentations from delegates from Germany followed by a break for half an hour and after that an hour of round-table discussions. At 7 we all take off for an hour of Urban Golf in Soho and then there's a medieval banquet at 9.30 at the Tower. Friday: we start with meetings to discuss and agree on next steps from half past nine till half eleven with coffee brought in to the meeting room and we then have a closing speech by the CEO for an hour which finishes at 12.30. Then there's a lunch at the Gay Hussars in Soho which goes on until 2 and after that a sightseeing tour of London for two hours. At four, for half an hour, there are farewell drinks and then departure to Heathrow.

Recycling key information

Sometimes we may have to explain a more complex concept or idea to our audience. One way of doing this is to restate the concept/idea in different words.

Recycling is achieved through:

▶ *Reformulation (saying something again in different words)*
"In other words ..."
"What I mean is ..."

▶ *Exemplification (giving clear examples of what you mean)*
"Let me give you an example ..."
"For example, ..."

▶ *Contextualisation (saying 'why' & 'how' things work)*
"The reason for doing X is ..."
"How do we do this? The answer is easy. We ..."

Example

You've just been asked to explain the meaning of 'Schadenfreude' (originally a German word which has been assimilated into the English language) to an international audience. You could say:

"What I mean by 'Schadenfreude' is finding humour in the misfortune of others. Let me give you a real-life example: Virgin tried to leverage its brand into the soft drinks market with Virgin Cola. The reason for entering the market was that, as you know, up until then Virgin had been successful in all of its businesses e.g., music and airline, and had a strong share of the 'cool' youth market and so there was no reason why it should fail with its Cola. However, it did – after initial success its popularity soon waned and is now only sold in cheap shops or on Virgin planes and trains. In the UK, we found it rather amusing that Virgin got it so very wrong. So, to sum up, 'Schadenfreude' means to find humour in someone else's misfortune."

The Q&A session

To inform or persuade through a presentation, you will need to deal effectively with the Q&A session. You can use the following expressions to ensure you understand what your questioner says.

Asking for repetition (you didn't hear)	I'm sorry, I didn't hear what you said/ Could you repeat the question, please?
Asking for repetition (you didn't understand)	I'm sorry, I'm not quite sure I understood the question/ Could you repeat the question, please?
Ensuring you understood the question correctly	So what you're asking is ... right?/ If I understand you correctly, you said ...
Ensuring you answered the question	I hope that answers your question/ Does that answer your question?

Delivery

How you say it is as important as what you say. Speak clearly – don't shout and don't whisper either. Don't speak too quickly or too slowly – pause at key points and stress key words to highlight the important information (have a look at chapter 4 to help you).

If you are nervous about giving a presentation, here are some voice warmers to help you to warm up your vocal chords and avoid that dreaded squeak.

Voice warmers

You can use the following exercises to build power and to warm up your voice before making a presentation:

- ▶ the siren – hum back and forth between the top and the bottom of your vocal range, like a siren. This will help you to vary your key and tone, making your voice sound more interesting and emphatic.

- ▶ the hum – to keep your voice from cracking unexpectedly during a presentation, warm up by humming a few bars of a song. Hum a sustained note for a count of 10, increase the volume for a count of 5 and, then, decrease it for a count of 5. This warms up your vocal cords.

- ▶ say this verse out aloud, focusing on precision and crisp consonants. This will help you to vary your rhythm and speed.

From The Night Mail by W H Auden

Letters of thanks, letters from banks
Letters of joy from girl and boy
Receipted bills and invitations
To inspect new stock or to visit relations,
And applications for situations,
And timid lovers' declarations,
And gossip, gossip from all the nations,
News circumstantial, news financial,
Letters with holiday snaps to enlarge in,
Letters for uncles, cousins, and aunts
Letters to Scotland from the South of France,
Letters of condolence to Highlands and Lowlands,
Notes from overseas to the Hebrides;
Written on paper of every hue,
The pink, the violet, the white and the blue,
The chatty, the catty, the boring, the adoring
The cold and official and the heart's outpouring,
Clever, stupid, short and long,
The typed, the printed and the spelt all wrong.

Final tips

Remember, most people are nervous before giving a presentation – let alone if it's in a foreign language. Try to avoid jokes – they simply don't travel. Use body language judiciously – don't wave your hands around too much and don't, whatever you do, put your hands in your pockets. Further, do look at your audience but don't focus on only one individual – it can be very intimidating for that person.

Finally, before you give a presentation – practise, practise, and practise again. Ask your friends/colleagues to listen to you and give you some feedback. If you feel it's valuable, take it on board.

11 Team building and giving/receiving feedback

Building effective teams across cultures involves taking on board and adapting to others' preferred working styles. You not only need to acquire strategies for dealing with different kinds of team players but you also need to be sensitive particularly when giving negative feedback.

Team roles

What is a team role? According to Belbin, a leading guru on team building, it is a "tendency to behave, contribute, and interrelate with others in a particular way." The value of Belbin's theory lies in gaining insight into how a team works and identifying its strengths and weaknesses. There are 3 action-oriented roles: shaper, implementer, and complete finisher; 3 people-oriented roles: coordinator, teamworker, and resource investigator; and 3 cerebral roles: plant, monitor evaluator, and specialist. The team roles are summarised in the table on the next page.

■ Task 1

Read the table which analyses the strengths and weaknesses of the roles and then find words in the table below that mean:

1. tend to
2. negative challenge
3. scrupulous
4. controlling someone or something to your own advantage
5. gets rid of
6. avoids
7. less important details
8. clear-sighted
9. spends too much time on

Team role		Strengths	Allowable weaknesses
Action oriented roles	**Shaper**	• Challenging, dynamic, thrives on pressure • The drive and courage to overcome obstacles	• Prone to provocation • Offends people's feelings
	Implementer (company worker)	• Disciplined, reliable, conservative and efficient • Turns ideas into practical actions	• Somewhat inflexible • Slow to respond to new possibilities
	Completer finisher	• Painstaking, conscientious, anxious • Searches out errors and omissions • Delivers on time	• Inclined to worry unduly • Reluctant to delegate
People oriented roles	**Co-ordinator** (Chairman)	• Mature, confident, a good chairperson • Clarifies goals, promotes decision-making, delegates well	• Can often be seen as manipulative • Offloads personal work
	Teamworker	• Co-operative, mild, perceptive and diplomatic • Listens, builds, averts friction	• Indecisive in crunch situations
	Resource investigator	• Extrovert, enthusiastic, communicative • Explores opportunities • Develops contacts	• Over-optimistic • Loses interest once initial enthusiasm has passed
Cerebral roles	**Plant**	• Creative, imaginative, unorthodox • Solves difficult problems	• Ignores incidentals • Too pre-occupied to communicate effectively
	Monitor evaluator	• Sober, strategic and discerning • Sees all options • Judges accurately	• Lacks drive and ability to inspire others
	Specialist	• Single-minded, self-starting, dedicated • Provides knowledge and skills in rare supply	• Contributes only on a narrow front • Dwells on technicalities

■ Task 2

Insert articles, a/an/the/or zero article, where appropriate in the text that follows. Have a look at Appendix D, page 164, for an overview of article usage.

(1) ... An ... ideal team should have (2) ... healthy balance of all (3) ... nine team roles. (4) ... strong teams normally have (5) ... coordinator, (6) ... plant, (7) ... monitor evaluator and one or more implementers, (8) ... teamworkers, resource investigators or completer finishers. (9) ... shaper should be (10) ... alternative to (11) ... coordinator rather than having both in the same team. In practice, (12) ... ideal is rarely (13) ... case and it can be helpful for (14) ... team to know which of (15) ... team roles are either overrepresented or underrepresented and to understand (16) ... individuals' secondary roles. (17) ... team roles tend to develop and mature and may even change with (18) ... experience and conscious attention. If (19) ... role is absent from (20) ... team, then it is often filled by someone who may not have recognized this role as (21) ... dominant one. (22) ... team should share their team roles to increase (23) ... understanding and enable (24) ... mutual expectations to be met.

Dealing with different team players

You are a member of a remote team of PAs from the same company working together to organize an international conference which will take place in the US next month. You have just been forwarded the two emails below from people in the remote team and your boss, who is the CEO, has asked you to solve the problem.

From: Carola Schmidt	To: Emily Mellow
Subject: Location of the conference next month	
Dear Emily As you may have heard, we have a problem with the conference venue – it's apparently been double-booked. I know I'm supposed to be organizing the location but I'm up to my eyes in work. As you are sorting out the equipment, it would make sense if you chose the venue too. Could you sort this out please? Regards Carola	

From: Emily Mellow	To: Carola Schmidt
Subject: Re Location of the conference next month	
Dear Carola I had heard that there was a problem but I'd prefer it if you could decide on the location. You have so much experience in organizing conferences and I really wouldn't know where to begin. There are so many venues to choose from. I am, however, still happy to help with the equipment unless you want to do this yourself? Thanks and best wishes Emily	

■ Task 3

Have another look at the table of team roles and identify a) the role and b) the allowable weaknesses of both Carola and Emily.

	Carola	Emily
Role		
Allowable weakness		

You now have to act as a go-between for Carola and Emily and insist politely that they fulfil their allotted tasks. You will probably also need to reassure them. Here are some expressions you can use:

Insisting:

▶ We all agreed that you would do ...
▶ You were happy to take on the job of ..., so could you please ...
▶ We all have a lot of work pressure so it would be good if you could ...

Reassuring by offering support:

▶ Rest assured that if you do ..., then X will take care of ...
▶ If you can sort out ..., then X will do ...
▶ We are all working on this as a team so if you could do ..., then X will be responsible for ...

■ Task 4

Write an email to Carola appealing to her strengths and asking her to choose the location. Reassure her that Emily will be responsible for arranging for the equipment needed.

■ Task 5

Write an email to Emily appealing to her strengths and confirming that she should arrange the necessary equipment in the conference room. Reassure her that Carola will be deciding on the location.

Feedback

When a team or indeed an individual wants to assess their effectiveness, they often look to feedback. Feedback should be verbal and where possible face-to-face or on the phone. Using email and other written forms of communication is not advisable as feedback is essentially two-way traffic.

Many people perceive feedback as criticism and, therefore, don't want to hear it. Others only want to be praised and reject anything that might smack of imperfection. Good team players, however, value and leverage objective feedback. This is not to say that we have to accept all feedback or the way in which it is delivered – we have the right to refuse feedback if it's not given in a respectful and supportive manner.

There are two sides to feedback – receiving it and giving it.

Receiving feedback

Claire, a secretary, has been given feedback by her immediate boss, a senior PA, on a recent meeting she organized. There were a few problems – the caterers were late, the LCD projector didn't work properly, and the room was too hot. The feedback was given with respect and face-to-face.

■ Task 6

Have a look at what Claire said in response and underline the expressions she used that are:

1. superficial – she listens and agrees but gives the impression that the feedback will have little effect on her

2. denial – she refutes the accuracy of the feedback

3. defensive – she defends her personal actions

4. attacking – she turns the tables on her boss

5. rationalizing – she finds explanations that absolves her of her responsibility

OK I hear what you're saying but I had very little time to organize everything ... if you'd told me about the meeting a month in advance instead of a week, I could have got things together much better. In any case, what you said isn't quite true – the projector did actually work, it's just that not all the participants could work it properly. And, as far as the caterers go – it really isn't my fault if they got lost and arrived half-an-hour late. I also really can't be held responsible for the weather and anyhow, it's the first time something like this has happened so I don't think I need worry too much about it.

■ Task 7

Contrast the previous response with the best-practice one below and underline expressions which are:

1. responsive – willing to hear what is being said without turning the tables on someone else

2. accepting – accepts the feedback without denial

3. engaged – interacts appropriately asking for clarification if necessary

4. interested – is genuinely interested in getting feedback

5. sincere – really wants to take changes on board

Thanks for taking the time to talk to me – it's always a learning curve for me to get feedback on an event. I know that things weren't perfect and I'd like to know what I can do to make it better next time. What I'd really like to know is what suggestions you've got that would ensure that, for example, the caterers arrive on time and that the room isn't too hot especially when I'm not on the spot.

Giving feedback

The other side of the coin is giving feedback – to be effective, you need to consider the content, the manner in which it is delivered, the timing, and the frequency with which you give it.

■ **Task 8**

Read this poor feedback message and analyse what's wrong with it:

You're really bugging the people in the customer service department – you're absolutely driving them mad. We've had the same problem with you again and again.

■ **Task 9**

Read this example of a feedback message – why is it more effective?

I'd like to talk to you about your relationship with the customer service department. Two members of staff called yesterday and said that you weren't very polite to them. Would you like to comment on that and tell me what happened?

N.B. When you give feedback:

▶ start with a strong opening (avoid er..er or um..um)

▶ stick to the facts (observations rather than interpretations)

▶ avoid giving mixed messages using words such as "however," "but," and "although"

▶ don't use negative and unspecific generalizations, such as "poor," "bad," "disappointing," etc.

▶ don't forget to use "thank you," where appropriate

■ **Task 10**

Your new junior wrote a good report which she presented to you yesterday. You want to give her positive feedback – what do you say?

Writing a Memo

Tips

A memo is a form of written communication used within an organisation. It generally contains no more than a single piece of information/request and usually asks for/ recommends action. Memos are not as formal as business letters and, therefore, the opening and closing phrases can be more direct and to the point. Use neutral language and apply the KISS (keep it short and simple) principle to sentence construction. The topic is normally introduced in the opening sentences and then moves on to supporting details – the body of the memo. This part of the memo is often presented in bullet points. Memos should not be longer than one page.

The heading

To:	(Readers' names and job titles)
From:	(Writer's name and job title)
Date:	
Subject:	(Be specific and concise)

You have received this email from your boss:

Dear Anne

As the company is growing so fast, I've decided to lay on some courses on team-building and feedback. Can you write a memo to the HR department and ask them to get in touch with some external consultants to find out about length and content of courses and how much they charge. This is pretty urgent and I also want them to get together a list of those people in the company who would benefit from the course in the first instance.

Thanks

Bill

■ Task 11

Write the memo in neutral language.

12 Deadlines and Reminders

The word *deadline* divides people into two groups, those who shrink and groan at the very mention of it and those who prick up their ears and feel their energy levels rising.

Think of a deadline as something positive; it provides a framework so that you know exactly how much time you have to do a particular task or work on a project. It helps you plan. Of course, a deadline must be realistic; if it is too tight, the quality of the work will probably suffer. Experience and planning will enable you to evaluate the feasibility of the deadline and if necessary, you may need to get the deadline extended or the workload reduced.

Asking to have deadlines extended or workload reduced

■ Task 1

Below are some useful sentences to use when negotiating for more time. Complete the gaps with a word/phrase from the box. The first one has been done as an example.

> calling in completed / draft / entails / hitches / meet / offload / reckon / slack / standards worked out

1. Having <u>worked out</u> exactly what this ...., I calculate that I'll need until the end of March to get a first .... to you.

2. I think we might have been too optimistic with our first deadline of March 20th. In order to complete the project to our usual high ...., I .... we need until the end of April.

3. Unless I can .... some of my other duties, I won't be able to get this .... until early April.

4. I would suggest .... some help here if we're to .... the March deadline.

5. Don't forget to plan to meet a deadline ahead of time. That way you will have some .... to work with in case there are any ....

Setting deadlines

You may find yourself managing a piece of work or a project where you are responsible for setting the deadline. If the project is complex, break down tasks into manageable chunks and set mini-deadlines. A series of mini-deadlines is a constructive way of keeping everyone's work on course and you can monitor progress. This way you will have plenty of warning if completion of the project looks as if it is going to be late. You can then either extend deadlines, or draft in help.

When issuing deadlines, be clear about why you have chosen a particular time period, and how it will benefit the project as a whole. Some of the phrases in the sentences that follow might be useful:

If we can get this new Website up and running by June, that'll give us July and August, our slack months, to deal with any teething troubles before we get into our hectic months, September and August.

I've checked with the team who worked on the X project, which was very similar to this one, and they estimate two months should be enough time for us to produce a first draft of the new brochure.

Looking at the extent of this project, I'd like to suggest we break it down into manageable parts. I believe we should have collected in all the data by the end of March. So that's the first milestone.

■ Task 2

Find phrases in the sentences above which mean

1. operating
2. problems which happen in the early stages
3. very busy
4. piece of text containing main ideas but not yet in its final form
5. size
6. divide into smaller units
7. important event

Getting people to stick to deadlines

This covers all sorts of areas of a PA's work, from getting projects or reports completed on time to getting clients to deliver goods or even pay their bills on time. The best way to avoid having to chase up people who have missed a deadline is to remind them about it beforehand. However, when a deadline arrives, and you have not received the report, payment or whatever it may be, your first port of call is to check whether it was made clear when the deadline was. This should have been clearly stated at the outset, when any work was commissioned, goods ordered or invoice sent. In the first reminder, you should make allowance for genuine mistakes, omissions, delays due to technology, etc.

If the work is an in-house report or something of that nature, you will probably talk to the person concerned directly.

Example

Hi Jack, Listen, I'm waiting for your report on X. I really need it because I'd like to feed the information in it into Friday's meeting with Sarah Trent.

■ Task 3

What would you say in the following situations?

1. You expected the travel itinerary for Mr. Nicolas Overbeek and Ms. Johanna Vatle by the end of the day yesterday. It is now 11am. Speak to Jeanette who is the member of your team who is responsible for producing the itinerary.

2. The deadline for Marc to have collated the information packs for delegates attending the conference is today. You see no evidence of this being done. Speak to Marc.

3. New stationery supplies are distributed to the offices on the 5th of every month. It is the 6th and your stock has not been replenished. Speak to Margot who is responsible for stationery supplies.

4. You asked Paul to draw up the office staff holiday planner for next year by the end of last week. You have not seen it yet. Talk to Paul.

Alternatively you might send an informal reminder by email.

Example

Dear Helen,

Could you let me have your report on X as soon as possible. I need time to go through it before Friday's meeting with Y. Do get back to me if there are any problems.

Many thanks

Hans

■ **Task 4**

Write an informal email to a colleague who was due to give you the first draft of an advertisement yesterday.

You should:

▶ ask whether the draft has been completed
▶ say why you need it (ad to go in next week's magazine)
▶ ask the colleague to contact you if there are problems
▶ set a deadline for today

Written reminders to clients

There are usually three stages taken by a supplier to recover a debt:

1. a polite letter which accepts there may be a good reason why the invoice has not been paid

2. a more insistent letter which:
   ▶ refers to the first polite letter
   ▶ has copies of invoices and statements enclosed
   ▶ specifies a date when you expect payment to be made by

3. a final demand which needs to be handled with tact as your objective is to recover the debt, not alienate the debtor. This final demand should:
   ▶ review the case so far
   ▶ specify how long the invoice has been outstanding for
   ▶ if necessary, threaten legal action if the invoice is not settled within a specified time

Example letter 1

First reminder

Request for payment

Dear Mr Belmont

I am writing with regard to our invoice No. YT 7832 for $6,843.58, a copy of which is enclosed. It would seem from our records that this invoice has not yet been settled.

In the past, you have always cleared your accounts regularly on the due dates. That is why I would like to ask if any problems have arisen which I may be able to help you with. Please let me know if I can be of any assistance.

Yours sincerely

Yann Tricard
Director

Enc. Invoice No. YT 7832

A terser letter could read as follows.

Example letter 2

Dear Sir,

Non-payment of invoice No. TH 8943 – 09

Unfortunately, it has come to our notice that payment of the above invoice, due 15th Dec 20XX, has not been received.

Please give this matter your immediate attention and transfer payment without delay.

Should the above invoice have already been paid, please disregard this reminder.

Yours faithfully,

Mark Thompson
Director

■ Task 5

Reply to example letter 1, explaining that the invoice has, in fact, now been paid, but there was a delay due to the introduction of a new finance software package in your system.

Example letter 3

Second reminder

Request for Payment

Dear Mr Gerard

With reference to my letter of 22nd September, I enclose copies of invoices which make up your July statement, the balance of which still remains outstanding.

Would you please either reply with an explanation as to why the balance of £2,668.65 has not been settled, or ensure that the account is cleared within the next seven days?

Yours sincerely

Jane Hervert
Credit controller

Encl.

■ Task 6

Write a second reminder to a company who has missed the deadline (June 5th) for printing some brochures you ordered (April 10th). You sent the first reminder June 8th.

> **Third and final demand for payment**
>
> *Dear Sir,*
>
> ***Invoice No. TH 8943 – 09***
>
> *Our records indicate that payment on your account is overdue to the amount of £5,460.00. A reminder was issued December 30th but we have as yet received no payment.*
>
> *If payment is not received by January 30th, I have no alternative but to refer this non-payment to our legal department. You can however, preserve your credit status with us by remitting your cheque today for the amount stated above.*
>
> *Yours faithfully,*

Hopefully, by setting realistic deadlines and keeping track of progress, we can ensure that deadlines are met and it is only the most severe of financial difficulties that will result in a letter such as the **Final demand!**

The language of deadlines and reminders

When we are discussing or writing about deadlines and reminders, we often express the idea of a condition. The condition is often expressed using *If ... ...,* .

Look at these sentences from the example letters, which express the idea of a condition.

1. Please let me know if I can be of any assistance.

2. Should the above invoice have already been paid, please disregard this reminder.

3. If payment is not received by January 30th, I have no alternative but to refer this non-payment to our legal department.

Notice that in sentence 2, *should* is a more formal way of saying *if*. These sentences are all examples of the zero conditional, i.e., they use a present tense in both parts of the sentence.

However, there are other forms which can be used, e.g., sentence 3 could be written in the first conditional form. The only difference in form is the use of a future tense in the second part of the sentence.

If payment is not received by January 30th, I will have no alternative but to refer this non-payment to our legal department.

If you would like to look at sample sentences and the structure of all the conditional forms in English, read Appendix D, page 167. You might like to do that before doing Task 7.

■ Task 7

There are four mistakes in the use of conditional forms in paragraphs 2, 3, and 6 in the article about stress. Find them and write the correct form.

If you feel you've got too much to do and too little time to do it in, you're probably stressed.

Your deadline is coming up and you haven't got any ideas. Your spouse smashed the car. The in-laws are coming for a week. Your boss is trying to close a big sale over the Internet and your computer crashes.

If this would sound familiar to you, you are almost certainly stressed out. Stress is constantly with us. What happens to you when you're under a lot of stress? Your heart races, your breathing gets faster, your blood circulation and metabolism speed up. Your muscles tense, getting you ready to fight or flee. But if you would not do either, it builds up.

Most people don't even realise they're stressed until they are about to reach boiling point. If something would have been done about it earlier, unpleasant symptoms such as headaches, hypertension, insomnia, and abdominal pain could have been avoided.

If you look someone straight in the eyes and see white under either iris or both, that person is under too much stress.

As soon as you realise you are under pressure you should:

1) *delegate tasks to others and trust them to get them done.*
2) *prioritise tasks. Do what must be done now.*
3) *take a break. Go for a walk or talk to someone.*
4) *do some exercise or some other fun activities.*
8) *do something totally different.*
9) *take deep breaths.*
10) *have a good laugh.*

80% of your worries never occur. If you could have done something about it, do it. If you can't do anything about it, don't let it bother you. Stress can best be managed by realising what you can change about your life and knowing what you can't.

13 Saying "no"

There are times when you want to say 'no' politely, times when you have to be more forceful in your refusal, and times when you really have to put someone in their place.

The degree of politeness versus assertiveness of a refusal depends not only on your relationship with the person who is asking you to do something but also on the attitude of the person who is asking. There are those who are sensitive and immediately recognise that you cannot do something, either because you have not got the time to do it or it is not your job to do it. On the other hand, there are those who are thick-skinned; they do not notice polite or indirect refusals or they simply think you are there to do their bidding whatever it may be!

Saying 'no' politely

To say 'no' politely in English we often begin with what may sound like an apology:

▶ *I'm sorry, you've come to the wrong person. You'll have to ask Renate to do that.* or,
▶ *I'm afraid I don't have the facts and figures to hand to be able to deal with that.*

We can use *I'm sorry* or *I'm afraid* followed by the reason why we cannot do something.

■ Task 1

Say 'no' politely in these situations.

1. Frank asks you to check that the fire exit notices are all correct and in place. This is not your job; Naomi is in charge of health and safety matters.

2. A pile of heavy boxes with photocopier paper has been left in the corridor. Sarah asks you to put them in the paper store. You have a bad back.

3. A colleague asks you if you could read through the minutes she took of a recent meeting before she distributes them. You simply do not have the time.

Different ways of saying 'no'

1. The direct 'no'

Sometimes, saying sorry, then saying no is not necessary or even appropriate. If that's the case, use the direct 'no'.

e.g.,

A: Are you joining us for lunch?
B: No, no thank you.

2. The reasoned 'no'

Sometimes you feel it would be polite to offer a reason for your refusal but, on the other hand, you don't want to open up any sort of negotiation. In this case, use the reasoned 'no'.

e.g.,

A: We're leaving now. Are you coming with us for a drink?
B: I can't come for a drink tonight. I've got to get this report out for tomorrow.

3. The reflecting 'no'

You want to acknowledge the request but still want to say 'no' quite firmly.

e.g.,

A: Do you have time to go through some things now?
B: I know you want to talk to me about the conference arrangements but I can't do it today.

4. The raincheck 'no'

This is similar to the reflecting 'no'. It's not so much saying 'no' as saying this is not a good time.

e.g.,

A: Could you check through these figures for me?
B: I can't right now, but I could some time tomorrow.

But be careful; only use this if you really do want to accept the request at a later date. Don't use it if you really mean 'no'

5. The unwavering 'no'

This is how you have to deal with pests – people who don't hear 'no'.

A: Come on let's go for lunch.
B: No, I'm not going out for lunch today
A: Oh, please, it won't take long.
B: No, I'm not going out for lunch today
A: Oh, go on, I'll pay.
B: No, I'm not going out for lunch today

■ Task 2

Match these ways of saying 'no' to the types 1 – 5 above. There may be more than one answer for some of the expressions.

a. *No can do right now, but what about Tuesday?*
b. *That's not possible today. It's my day to get the monthly stats out.*
c. *No, no thank you.*
d. *No, it's not my scene.*
   No, really, it's not my scene.
e. *I can see it would be helpful to crosscheck with someone, but I can't put this report aside right now.*

Saying 'no' politely is not usually a problem among colleagues especially if you can say it face-to-face because friendly body language can go a long way to softening any refusal. However, when dealing with clients and other business contacts over the phone, the phrases and tone of the voice used have to meet the norms of the listener's culture. Generally, a low voice, the use of words linked together, and a measured pace rather than a high staccato voice are well-received.

Saying 'no' more firmly

Imagine this scenario:

Beate: *The representatives from Wilson & Co have decided to drop by on their way to the airport this afternoon. They just want to go through the latest draft of the proposal with Jorge and me. Could you just get some cakes or something like that for 6 people when you're out on your lunch break?*

Background: This is not the first time Beate has unexpectedly asked you to do something during your lunch break. Moreover, there is a system for ordering catering supplies which you do when required by phone with a local company. You have in the past done as Beate asked but you notice that this situation is arising more and more frequently. The last time you pointed out to her that you would prefer to be notified in advance of catering requirements and that an extra stock of non-perishable items could be kept for 'emergencies", she basically took no notice of your suggestion and seems to treat you increasingly casually.

You: *Beate, I don't wish to sound unhelpful but as this has come up again, I really must point out that my lunch breaks are exactly that – my lunch breaks and if I'm needed to go out on office business, I'd prefer it to be done in office time. But that shouldn't be necessary, anyway. As I suggested before, we need to have a system where we keep some things for times like this so that no one has to give up precious office time 'to run an errand'. I'll call the deli and get them to send some cakes round. It's a very expensive way of doing it but I'm really too busy to go out now and I'd rather not use my lunchtime for office business.*

Beate: *Well, try and call the deli and see if they can deliver what we need today. If not, could you go to lunch early and pick up what you order?*

You: *Yes, and should I order some things to keep by?*

Beate: *Yes, good idea.*

■ Task 3

Complete the dialogue below with appropriate words or phrases from the box. There are two phrases which do not fit.

A.	but that shouldn't be necessary, anyway
B.	you've asked me to pick up the pieces
C.	I really must point out that
D.	why don't you find out where the problem lies
E.	but aren't you the best person to deal with that

Background: Paula is responsible for organising your company's attendance at a trade fair. You have had nothing whatsoever to do with the arrangements. Paula is prone to offloading work, especially when problems start appearing, and you really want to discourage this.

Paula: *I've just been looking at the map of the trade fair and notice that our name is not next to our stand. Could you look into it? I'm not sure where the problem lies, with the printers, the trade fair organisers ...*

You: *I'm sorry, (1) .... as you've been in charge of all the arrangements for that trade fair?*

Paula: *Well, I'm really snowed under with work at the moment so could you just chase up what's happened about the map?*

You: *Actually, Paula, this isn't the first time (2) .... when things start to go wrong, and I think you should follow this up yourself. (3) .... and then take it from there?*

Paula: *Well, OK, but I don't know how I'm going to find time to do everything. (walks away)*

Saying 'no' assertively

Two of the most common complaints among PAs are:

▶ I'm expected to work overtime and this is not stated in my contract.
▶ I'm expected to do many tasks that are not in my job description.

If you are working in these conditions, it is likely that resentment will build up against the boss, the job, and even the company. Therefore, it is imperative that you air your views and get the situation changed.

If you notice that your polite refusals have turned into lies, e.g., *Oh, I'm sorry, I have to pick a friend up from the station at 7 tonight*, it is time to set up a meeting with your line manager. You could do this by saying:

I'd like to put aside 30 minutes this week so that I can express some concerns I have.

By arranging an appropriate time and determining the length of time of the meeting, you can plan what you want to say and how you are going to say it.

> ### Example
>
> At the meeting:
>
> You: *Thank you for putting aside some time. I'd like to talk about two concerns I have. The first is that I find I am increasingly being asked to work overtime. This isn't in my contract and I'd rather not do it as I enjoy a balance between home life and work.*
>
> Boss: *Well, you know, sometimes we just have to get a document out for a client that night – what else can we do?*
>
> You: *Before we go into that, I'd like to outline my second concern and that is that I'm being asked to do jobs which aren't in my job description.*
>
> Boss: *Well, there's always a bit of give and take ...*
>
> You: *If you'd let me finish. The second concern impacts on the first in that as I'm doing more tasks, the total workload can't be achieved within the working day. So, in order to avoid this happening, I've made a list of the tasks which are not within my remit and that I shouldn't be asked to do.*

Remember:

▶ arrange a dedicated time to discuss your concerns; this highlights the importance of the matter

▶ remain courteous and calm

▶ acknowledge your boss's views but stick to your stock phrases which express your concerns clearly and concisely

▶ don't be bullied

■ **Task 4**

Highlight phrases in the dialogue above which show that

1. you are being courteous
2. you do not want to be sidetracked from expressing your second concern
3. you have more to say
4. you have thought of a solution

■ **Task 5**

Write an email to your line manager setting up a meeting to discuss some issues which you are unhappy with.

Reporting unacceptable behaviour

Unacceptable behaviour can take many forms: bullying, sexual harassment, sexual or racial discrimination, to mention but a few. It can make an employee's life a misery, lead to stress-related illnesses, and affect their performance and damage careers

The following guidelines are useful when an employee is experiencing unacceptable behaviour. They have been drawn up for employees working in European or North American companies. Of course, the steps a person can take when unacceptable behaviour occurs, depends on the business culture surrounding the incident.

Guidelines

▶ If someone harasses you, try to tell them that you do not like their behaviour and that you want them to stop. You might want to ask one of your colleagues, or your union representative – someone you feel you can trust – to accompany you to give you moral support. If necessary, they could also act as a witness.

▶ If you feel you can't face the harasser, you might prefer to write to them to explain that their behaviour is upsetting you and to ask them to stop. Let them know that you will take the matter further if they carry on. It's useful to keep a copy of the letter.

▶ Note down all the behaviour that offends you in a diary. Record the date, time, and place, and the names of any other people who are there. This will help you to remember details if you decide to make a complaint.

▶ If the harassment is affecting your health, for example, causing symptoms of stress or depression, go to see your doctor.

▶ Report the harassment to your employer. You could go to your HR department (if there is one) and ask what your company's procedures are for reporting a grievance. Alternatively, go to your union representative (if there is one). Make a record of the date you complained about the harassment, who you spoke to, what was said, and what action was agreed on. This will be important if you decide later that you want to go to an employment tribunal.

▶ Whoever you report to should make certain that your complaint is investigated and that something is done about it.

■ Task 6

Find words or phrases in the guidelines above which mean:

1. makes someone unhappy or anxious by causing them problems

2. an organisation of workers from a particular profession which represents and protects the rights of the workers

3. approval and encouragement

4. a person who sees an event happening, especially a crime or accident

5. upsets or hurts someone's feelings

6. signs of illness or physical or mental changes which are caused by a disease

7. complaint or strong feeling that you have been treated unfairly

8. special court dealing with problems to do with work

Letter to a harasser

■ Task 7

In the second bullet point in the guidelines, it is suggested that a letter could be written to a harasser if speaking to them is difficult. Complete the letter below with suitable phrases from the box.

---

constitute / does / direct / directly / find / making / nature / point / such / take

---

Dear Mr. Timpson

I am writing to (1) .... out to you that I (2) .... one aspect of your behaviour towards me unacceptable; that is, the comments of a sexual (3) .... which you (4) .... towards me. For example, yesterday afternoon, when I was picking up a piece of paper from the floor, you said, couldn't you do that again, I love a bit of leg.

I find comments (5) .... as these very upsetting and I believe they (6) .... sexual harassment. I am asking you to stop (7) .... such comments either (8) .... to me or indirectly about me.

If this behaviour (9) .... continue, I will have no alternative but to (10) .... the matter further.

Yours sincerely

■ Task 8

Imagine that a colleague has asked for your help to draft a letter to her harasser. She has a male colleague who constantly tries to put her down. He frequently makes comments to the effect that she is stupid because she is a woman, and a blonde woman at that!

Draft a letter to Mr. Vozenko for your colleague.

Harassment report to manager

A company may have a complaints report form that will guide you through what you have to note down when reporting your grievance. Generally, this will ask you to detail:

▶ who the harasser is
▶ what happened and when
▶ how this has affected you
▶ who witnessed it
▶ what steps you have taken to have this behaviour stopped

If your company does not have such a form, you could write a report using those same headings. This makes sure the report keeps to the facts. It is inadvisable to show emotion.

■ Task 9

Look at this first draft of a harassment report form. How would you improve it and adapt it to your work situation?

Report of harassment

Department . . . .

Date . . . .

Name of person reporting harassment . . . .

Name of person complained about . . . .

Name of line manager . . . .

Nature of harassment . . . .

Details of incident: Date: _____ *Time:* _____ *Place:* _____

What happened? . . . .

. . . .

. . . .

. . . .

. . . .

Who witnessed the incident? . . . .

14 Writing CVs with impact, covering letters, and letters of reference

A Curriculum Vitae (CV) provides a prospective employer with a summary of your professional life. It lists your achievements – both educationally and in terms of your experience. Prospective employers use CVs and/or covering letters to decide whom they will interview. As CVs are your first introduction to a new company, it means that it's worth getting them as near perfect as possible.

How do you prepare to write a CV?

Your CV is your own personal marketing tool. This tool is your opportunity to sell yourself to prospective employers. It should include details of your personal qualities, skills, achievements, education, and work experience. You should, therefore, make notes on all the factual information you need together with dates, grades, etc. before you actually start writing your CV.

If you are responding to a job advertisement, read it very carefully and highlight the skills, experience, and qualifications it asks for. You can then target those skills that you have specifically at the job requirements.

■ Task 1

Read the following text and match the headings a – e to their descriptions 1 – 7.

a. Additional information
b. People who can vouch for you
c. Work experience
d. Attainments
e. Personal details
f. Hobbies
g. Education

How do you write a CV?

A CV is divided into headings so that readers can tell where one piece of information ends and another begins. The reader should not be confronted by an endless disordered river of information which is difficult to make head or tail of. International CVs are usually ordered as follows:

1. name, address, telephone number, mobile number, email address, date of birth, nationality, marital status

2. dates of schools/colleges/universities attended together with subjects studied and qualifications and grades obtained. Begin with the most recent.

3. start with the most recent or current job. Give the dates you were employed (year and/or month and year) and the name and address or city of the firm. Give a short account of your responsibilities.

4. give brief information on your specific achievements. These should generally be work-related but could include, for example, running a first-aid course or ensuring health and safety regulations are adhered to. They are usually non-academic.

5. provide any further information that could support your job application. For example, ability to speak foreign languages.

6. give examples of your interests etc. Be careful not to include too many that are of an individualistic nature but also try to list, for example, sports that require you to be a team player.

7. obviously you need to ask the person/people concerned first! Normally all you need to put here is 'References can be supplied on application'.

N.B. A CV is generally one side of A4, maximum 2 A4 pages.

Sample CV

CURRICULUM VITAE

Name:	Anne Smith
Address:	35 Arundel Close, Bristol BL6 2RJ, UK
Telephone:	01793 562451
Mobile:	07788 069531
Email:	a.smith@tonline.com
Date of Birth:	23/10/1973
Education	1994 – 1995 Pitmans College, London 1991 – 1994 Bangor University, Wales 1984 – 1991 Bristol Community College
Qualifications:	1995 Diploma in Secretarial Studies, Advanced Level 1994 BA Degree in History of Art, 2:1 1991 A Levels in Art, English, & Information Technology
Work experience:	2000 – Present PA to Human Resources Director, Corus, London 1998 – 2000 Secretary to Sales Manager, Virgin Superstore, Crawley, Sussex 1996 – 1998 Secretary to Financial Advisor, Barclays Bank, plc
Achievements:	2002 Worked with HR manager on new appraisal system, Corus 2000 Devised new method for production of quarterly sales figures 1997 Implemented a new filing system for Barclays Bank, Bristol branch
Additional information:	Foreign languages: Spanish: Advanced Portuguese: Intermediate Arabic: False Beginner Currently studying for an Open University Distance Learning Programme in HR Management
Interests and Hobbies:	Hang-gliding, travelling, basketball, painting, travelled round the world 1995 – 1996
References:	Can be supplied on application

Dos and don'ts when you write a CV

■ **Task 2**

What are the dos when you write a CV? For example:

▶ order it logically
▶
▶
▶
▶
▶

■ **Task 3**

What are the don'ts when you write a CV? For example:

▶ include every minor qualification you have
▶
▶
▶
▶
▶

Covering letters

The covering letter you send with your CV should briefly highlight the special strengths, skills, and experience you have for the job you're applying for. The letter should consist of:

▶ your address

▶ the first/last name of addressee (if known)

▶ their position/title

▶ company name

▶ address

▶ opening: Dear Ms/Mr/Dr X or Dear Sir/Madam

▶ the first paragraph should refer to the job you're applying for and where you saw the advertisement

▶ the second paragraph should begin by stating that you are enclosing your CV. It should focus on the qualifications or experience you have which make you an attractive candidate for the position

▷ the third paragraph should state your readiness to attend an interview and how the interviewer can contact you

▷ closing: Yours sincerely/Yours faithfully depending on how you began the letter

▷ your signature and name printed underneath

■ Task 4

The sentences in the body of this letter of application are jumbled up. Put them in the right order by numbering the sentences 1 – 6.

---

33 Belgrave Square
London SW3 4BX

Design Centre International
28 Twickenham Street
London SW1 5QL

February 8 20XX

Dear Sir/Madam,

a) *I am enclosing a copy of my curriculum vitae which gives details of my qualifications and experience.*

b) *My contact numbers are fixed line: 01208 37254 and mobile: 07784 0365932.*

c) *Although I did not need to travel in my previous job, I would be most willing to do so.*

d) *I am writing in response to your advertisement for a Personal Assistant to the Marketing Manager in yesterday's Guardian.*

e) *I will be available for interview at any time convenient to you.*

f) *As you will see, I have had ten years' experience in a similar business environment and have a Diploma as a PA from the London Chamber of Commerce.*

I look forward to hearing from you.

Yours faithfully,

Christina Green

Christina Green
Enc.

■ **Task 5**

What advice would you give someone on how to write a covering letter?

Dos:

▶

▶

▶

▶

Don'ts:

▶

▶

▶

Finally, your CV and covering letter give you the opportunity to shine – so do so!

Writing a letter of reference

The employment market is highly competitive and a letter of recommendation may well make all the difference between an applicant being offered a job or turned down for it.

If you are asked to write a letter of reference, the rule of thumb is: if you can't find anything good to say about the person, then it's better not to say anything at all. In other words, if all you have to say are negative things, then decline the invitation to write the letter and suggest someone else who may have more positive things to say.

Tips for writing a letter of reference

▶ make sure the letter is well-presented. A dog-eared piece of paper will reflect badly on you and on the person you're writing the letter for

▶ write it on headed paper

▶ include your professional relationship to the person – were you their team leader/ boss/ supervisor etc.?

▶ give honest fact-based information. Don't be vague or wishy-washy

▶ highlight their skills, responsibilities, attitude, personal attributes, and their contribution to the performance of your company

▶ avoid using bland words, such as *nice, good, satisfactory, decent* etc. Use words which have more impact, such as *effective, efficient, articulate, intelligent, cooperative, innovative, flexible, dependable* etc.

▶ include characteristics of the person that will make them attractive to a prospective new employer, such as *fluency in foreign languages, self-confidence, willingness to go the extra mile, initiative, leadership, ability to handle conflict* etc.

▶ remember to write the letter promptly because a job offer may depend on receiving the letter on time

■ Task 6

Find words or expressions in the text above which are similar in meaning to:

1. of book/papers used so much that the corners are turned down
2. not having clear or firm ideas
3. insipid
4. prepared to do more to ensure the job is properly done

Structuring a letter of reference

▶ headed paper with company name and address

▶ addressee name and address if known

▶ date

▶ salutation – *Dear Sir/Madam, Dear Mr/Ms X*, or if you have no name *To Whom It May Concern*

▶ confirm dates/job title

▶ explain the person's responsibilities

▶ describe the person's performance, attitude, and skills

▶ end the letter – *Yours faithfully* if you begin with Dear Sir/Madam or *Yours sincerely* if you're writing to a named addressee

Remember that it's up to you as to how much positive information and praise you include in your letter.

■ **Task 7**

Insert the appropriate prepositions, e.g., at, in, on etc. into the letter below.

Sample letter

Fly-on-the-Wall plc
32 Audley Street
Cambridge CB1 4JN

HR Department
Macrosystems plc
2 London Wall
London EC1 4GE

November 21, 20XX

To Whom It May Concern

I am the Head (1) .... the PR division (2) .... Fly-on-the-Wall plc and confirm that Susanne Robinson was employed as a PA with us (3) .... April 20XX (4) .... October 20XX. Her position carried the following responsibilities – she was a team leader of five junior secretaries and was also my PA. During her four years with us, she ensured that the administrative function of the department ran smoothly and demonstrated her commitment (5) .... the company (6) .... numerous occasions. She was a supportive mentor (7) .... her staff, has outstanding interpersonal skills, and was always efficient and effective (8) .... managing her tasks. Her work was (9) .... a consistently high standard and her good knowledge (10) .... French and German proved invaluable (11) .... our foreign clients.

I, therefore, have no hesitation (12) .... recommending her (13) .... the position (14) .... PA (15) .... the CEO of Macrosystems plc.

Yours faithfully

Frederick Ashton
Head of PR

You may sometimes be asked to provide a letter of reference of a more personal nature, commenting on a person's suitability to e.g., work for a charity or join a foundation etc. The same ground rules apply – only state the positives with a particular slant as to why and for whom you're writing the reference.

Sample personal reference

111 Winston Road
London SE11 4PP

Dr Mark Coolie
Save the Children
100 Piccadilly
London W1 7SB

November 30, 20XX

Dear Dr Coolie

I have known Johanna Carsten for 10 years in both a business and social capacity. We have, in fact, worked together for the past 3 years on a voluntary basis raising funds to establish a daycare centre for disadvantaged children. I have found her to be utterly reliable, dependable, and fully committed to improving the quality of life for these children.

Moreover, she has been acting as an unpaid bookkeeper for the charity and has, at all times, been completely trustworthy and conscientious in handling our funds.

I would, therefore, recommend her heartily as a valuable addition to the Board of your organisation.

Yours sincerely

Marsha Green

15 Conference invitations and requests for abstracts, cards for various occasions

Organising a conference

When inviting speakers or delegates to a conference you're organising, you need to make sure the person gets all the information they require. You may put this information on your Website and/or you may directly mail or email particular individuals.

■ Task 1

Brainstorm the information needed by speakers or delegates.

▶ Letter of invitation
▶

General information

▶
▶
▶
▶

Registration

▶
▶
▶
▶

Engaging speakers

Organisers can recruit speakers either by invitation or by a call for papers. In either case, action should be taken well ahead of the planned event: a lead-in time of one year should normally be thought of as a minimum.

Call for papers and abstracts

■ Task 2

Complete the Call for Papers and Abstracts template with words from the box.

---

accompanied / acknowledge / contribute / including / cover / likely / presented /
queries / submit / underway

Call for Papers

Planning for the 20XX ABC Technical Conference is already (1) .... and again we are seeking ideas, speakers and sponsors.

We invite speakers on all types of XXX development to (2) .... The programme will (3) .... a variety of subjects, including XXX. Any topic (4) .... to be of interest to Linnel developers and enthusiasts will be considered.

The topics (5) .... in recent years have included: ....

...

...

More information about previous events can be found at: (list Websites).

Abstracts

Abstracts for the conference should be (6) .... by a short biography and, ideally, should be about 250-500 words long. Final papers should normally last about 45 minutes, (7) .... 10 minutes for questions and answers. If you need more time for your presentation, please tell us when you (8) .... your abstract.

Abstracts should be submitted to the conference organisers electronically through this form (Web link).

We shall (9) .... all submissions.

Significant Dates

Closing date for abstracts .... 29 March 20XX
Accepted authors notified by ...... 18 April 20XX
Final papers due by .... 17 June 20XX

Particular (10) .... should be sent either to (office address), or to the 20XX programme committee (email address)

Letter of invitation to a conference speaker

■ **Task 3**

The first paragraph of the letter of invitation below is in the correct place. However, the subsequent paragraphs have been jumbled up. Put them into the correct order by writing the numbers 2 – 8 next to the appropriate paragraph.

NB. There are two paragraphs after the closing salutation.

Dear ***,

I am writing to you in my capacity as Program Committee Co-Chair for the 18th Annual Computational Linguistics Conference, to be held in Hong Kong, October 1–8, 20XX. As you may know, the ACL conference is the premier international conference of note in the field of computational linguistics and natural language processing. I am writing to ask whether you would be willing to present a talk at the conference as an invited speaker. Invited talks will be one hour long, including a 10 minute question & answer session.

I will be away for an extended period and will not be able to read my email on a regular basis during this time. So please cc Professor Ida Grenville, an area chair and member of the ACL-20XX program committee, in your response. She has kindly agreed to coordinate the invited speaker sessions during my absence.

PS If you accept our invitation to give an invited talk at the conference, you can choose to write a paper up to 8 pages long that will be included in the conference proceedings. Along with the paper hard copy, we request you provide a PDF file for inclusion in the CD-ROM version of the proceedings. If you choose to write a paper, please provide the hard copy and PDF file by August 1st. Please visit the conference Webpage (http://www.cs.ust.hk/acl20XX) and click on "Instructions for Authors" for specific details on the formatting and submission of the camera-ready papers.

Regardless of whether you choose to provide a paper for the proceedings, we request you to provide us a title and an abstract (up to 200 words) by August 1st, 20XX.

We have not yet established on which day your talk would be scheduled; should you accept this invitation, there is some flexibility we can use to accommodate your own scheduling preferences (although it would be on one of the main conference session days, Tuesday October 3 through Friday October 6).

I do very much hope that you will be able to accept this invitation.

In appreciation of your agreement to provide an invited talk, ACL would provide the cost of an economy class airfare from your home institution to the conference, hotel accommodation during the conference, and free registration to the conference.

Yours sincerely

***

Writing cards – useful phrases for various occasions

It often falls to the PA to buy the card and the present or flowers for someone's leaving do, retirement party or stay in hospital. So you rush around, consult colleagues, check on how much 'spending power' you've got, and go out and make the agonising choice. And running through the back of your mind, you're wondering whether they will just love this gift or will they think 'What is it?' or 'Why on earth would I want one of those?'. But then you've got to write the card. Isn't it strange how words can just fail you at that moment? Fear not. Help is at hand.

Get well cards

So, you're almost ready to send out that get-well flower delivery but you're stuck for words as to what to write on the card. It's OK; we're not all the creative type. In addition, a get-well card can be a difficult thing to write. The important thing is that the card and its message should fit the person.

■ Task 4

Match the get-well card messages below to these two types of people. Choose two messages for each person.

People

A. a young bubbly woman, in a junior position at work, who broke her leg on a skiing holiday

B. a man in his 60s who is reserved, and in quite a high position at work, who is at home but suffering from whiplash after a car accident

Get well messages

1. Wishing you a speedy recovery.
2. We miss you at the office! Get well soon.
3. Our thoughts are with you, hope you feel better soon.
4. Hope these brighten your room and cheer you up.

Here are some other phrases that you could use or adapt to fit the situation:

▶ We need you at the office. Come back soon.
▶ I hope you're back on your feet soon.
▶ Sending you all the healing thoughts in the world.
▶ Sending you sunshine and cheer!
▶ I hope this brightens your day!

▶ We miss you! Hurry back!
▶ Hope you feel better soon.

Cheering someone up

Sometimes we know someone is just down and needs cheering up. A little card with a message could mean a lot. Here are some expressions you can use.

▶ Cheer up
▶ Thinking of you!
▶ May things get better soon.
▶ Sending sunny thoughts to brighten your day.
▶ Hope this brightens your day!
▶ I hope these ruin a perfectly bad day! (only suitable for someone who enjoys being miserable and who has a dry sense of humour)

Sympathy cards

When someone has died, it can be particularly difficult to find the words to add to a sympathy card or note to attach with flowers. We are often at a loss for words and it's normal not to know what to say. Your support is important though, so you need to try to express your feelings and those of colleagues. The two principle situations that can arise are: a colleague has died, or a family member or close friend of a colleague has died. You will need to know if the person you're writing to and the deceased are of any particular religion before you write your message.

■ Task 5

Put a tick next to the phrases which may be particularly suitable for a religious family.

▶ Our sympathies for your loss.
▶ You and your family are in our prayers.
▶ Martha will be sadly missed.
▶ Alex touched our lives and will be missed.
▶ You are in our thoughts and prayers.
▶ You are in our hearts during this difficult time.
▶ Rachel's memory will live on forever.
▶ We are so sorry for your loss.
▶ James will live in our hearts forever.
▶ We share your sorrow.
▶ Thinking of you in these difficult times.

New baby cards

Turning to happier occasions, you may need to send a card to a colleague or spouse of a colleague who has just had a baby. Messages to new mothers and fathers tend to fall into two categories: joyous and humorous.

■ Task 6

Use a preposition to fill in the gaps in these messages.

Joyous

1   *Congratulations .... the birth .... your first baby girl!*

2   *We share .... the celebration of the birth .... your baby boy.*

3   *Congratulations .... you and Mike, and enjoy the years together.*

4   *Another miracle .... this world. Welcome!*

Humorous

5   *Don't worry, you'll get used .... sleepless nights! And he's worth it!*

6   *All good things come .... little bundles. Congratulations!*

7   *And then there were three. We're all looking forward .... seeing the little one .... Friday.*

8   *A big welcome .... the new addition .... your family!*

Congratulations

There are many other occasions when you may wish to send a card congratulating a colleague on something, e.g., passing an exam. Remember the language structure after *congratulations* is *to someone on something*.

Congratulations on passing your accountancy exams.

If you'd like to be less formal, the following phrases might be suitable:

▶ This calls for a celebration.
▶ Congratulations – you did it!
▶ I knew you'd pass – honest!
▶ *Will you still talk to us now that you're DOCTOR Fewtrell?

*Remember that humour does not always cross cultures.

Work anniversaries

When someone has been working in a company for a significant number of years, 10, 20, 30 etc, there is usually a ceremony to mark the occasion.

■ Task 7

Tick the messages which you would have to use with caution, e.g., if you don't know the person very well.

▶ Congratulations on this great achievement. All the best.
▶ How can someone who looks 40 have worked somewhere for 30 years?
▶ Wow! That's really something!
▶ 20 years – you mad fool!
▶ Congratulations! And here's to the next 10.
▶ Congrats! Do you get a medal?
▶ Congratulations on a memorable 15 years.

Retirement cards

Sometimes it's easy to know what to put for the first line of a message, but then you feel you should follow it up with something more personal. And that can be tricky.

■ Task 8

Add another more personal line to these messages.

1. *Congratulations on your retirement.*
2. *So, you're retired? Just think of all the things you can do with all that free time!*
3. *Happy retirement! We're going to miss you.*
4. *Best wishes on your retirement.*

Do you like this one?
The beginning of Do-as-U-like days!

New job cards

It's inevitable that colleagues will come and go, so cards and gifts for people leaving to go to a new job are quite common. This can be a tricky situation too as you don't want the message on the card to suggest anything negative about the present company. So cards with main messages like *The Great Escape* might not be suitable.

▶ You landed your dream job!
▶ Rich 'n Famous
▶ Sailing in new waters
▶ Your big break

Also don't forget that messages that rhyme can be seen as rather cheesy, e.g.,

Best wishes as you begin your new job.
As each new gate opens and pathways unfold
May you find the best of all things
That a lifetime can hold.

Thank-you cards/notes

There are times when you want to say thank you to someone in the company. This might be someone who is in a superior position to you or someone who is in a lower grade post.

■ Task 9

Match the beginnings and endings of these messages. There are two possible endings for 1 and 6.

1.	Your advice and motivation ...	A.	... encouragement and support.
2.	Thank you for entrusting me ...	B.	... are really appreciated today and all the year.
3.	Thank you for your ...	C.	... have been invaluable. Thank you.
4.	Thanks for being on ...	D.	... great work!
5.	Keep up the ...	E.	... with the Spylaw contract. All I have to do now is live up to your expectations!
6.	Your hard work and dedication ...	F.	... my team. Good job!

16 Influencing strategies and tactics

There are many occasions when we want to influence people so that they accept our point of view, pursue a course of action or simply give their consent or support for something. The article that follows outlines the most common influencing strategies and tactics.

■ Task 1

Find words or expressions in the article below which mean:

a. carefully/sensibly
b. getting someone to agree to participate
c. be careful of
d. menacing
e. bullying
f. deceiving
g. horrible
h. complains
i. does nothing
j. has the courage to do something

How to influence people and win friends

Influencing has two sides – the positive and the negative. Always try to use the former and use the latter judiciously. Most jobs require you to influence others at some point or another. This could range from getting someone on board for a project, persuading someone to see things the way you see them, or even asking your boss for a rise or promotion. First and foremost, to be a good influencer you need excellent interpersonal and communication skills – you need to know which strategy will work with whom. Researchers in the field have identified six common influencing strategies and their accompanying tactics.

Strategies	Tactics
Explaining	Legitimising Logical persuasion
Asking	Appealing to friendship Socialising Consulting
Stating	Stating
Inspiring	Appealing to values Modelling
Exchanging	Exchanging
Alliance building	Alliance building

In fact, alliance building is regarded as a macro-strategy because it can involve a mix of different strategies and tactics to influence others.

Strategies and tactics explained

But what exactly do these strategies and tactics mean and how can we apply them linguistically?

Strategies	Tactics	Expressions
Explaining means giving reasons for what you want	• Legitimising – using authority • Logical persuasion – using facts/logic	• According to company policy ... • The facts speak for themselves
Asking means exactly that or making a request	• Appealing to friendship – asking a personal favour • Socialising – building rapport • Consulting – asking for input	• Would you do me a favour and ... • I hear you spent a year in the US – I did too – when were you there? • Would you like to tell us about your ideas on ...
Stating means saying what you want or think	• Making a direct but polite statement	• This report has to be finished by tomorrow

Strategies	Tactics	Expressions
Inspiring means affecting behaviour by emotion or example	• Appealing to values – being motivational • Modelling – setting or leading by example	• We all need to work our hardest and best to be in the top 3 • What I've learnt from experience is that if we do X in this way, ...
Exchanging means trading something valuable to get support	• Exchanging favours/ benefits	• If you help me with ..., I'll give you a hand with ...
Alliance building	• Alliance building means getting others on your side to help influence someone	• We are part of the same team so shouldn't we all be ... • We really need to pull together to achieve ...

Negative tactics – beware how you use them!

There are also four negative tactics which can be effective but should be used sparingly as they will damage a relationship. They are: *avoiding* which is failing to act or respond and thus reserving the right to say "I told you so!" when things go wrong; *threatening* which is expressing anger and being aggressive and saying things, such as "If you don't do X, then I'll make damn sure you don't get Y!"; *intimidating* which is using power to get your own way if you are in the up position and being rude and insensitive, for example, "What do you know, you've only been here five minutes!"; and *manipulating* which can include having a hidden agenda and deliberately lying or misleading someone. Obviously, these tactics are needed occasionally, for example, to shut up a particularly obnoxious person but they won't win you any friends and should be avoided at all costs if you want to maintain the relationship.

Good influencers are fun to be around

Finally, something to bear in mind is that people like being around good influencers because they are movers and shapers and make things happen. Think about it, who would you rather be with – someone who moans about things all the time and sits on their hands or someone who puts their head above the parapet and gets things moving along for everyone's benefit?

■ **Task 2**

Respond to the situations below using any influencing strategy and accompanying expressions you feel comfortable with. In real life, of course, we don't just stick to one strategy or tactic but mix and match them depending on the circumstances.

1. *You arrived late at a hotel last night which is often used by your company. You are attending a conference which you helped organise – this is very hard work and you desperately need a good night's sleep. However, the hotel is full of very loud football fans who are partying long into the night. What do you say to the hotel manager when you telephone him?*

2. *It is Friday lunchtime. You have arranged a weekend away with your family and want to leave early. Your boss has just sent you an email asking you to rewrite his entire presentation which he needs first thing on Monday morning. You know this will take several hours. What do you say in your email?*

3. *It is 6pm and you are just about to leave the office when you receive a voicemail from your colleague in the US.*
   "Hi Ramona, this is Jenny from the New York office. You know that meeting we were planning for next week in New York for all European department heads – well it's been cancelled because my boss is ill. Can you let your people know please asap. I'm waiting for your call – thanks."
   What do you say when you leave her a voicemail?

You will be more effective at influencing people if you adapt your tactics to their MBTI type. Read the following text to find out what MBTI type you are and how to recognise the characteristics of other MBTI types.

The Myers Briggs Type Indicator (MBTI)

Dealing with difficult people is one thing but have you ever wondered why you seem to relate better to some people than others? Why some of your colleagues seem to be on your wavelength whereas others have very different thought processes and styles? Have you ever asked yourself "Why don't they get it?" when an idea, conclusion or plan of action seems *obvious* to you? The MBTI is a widely used instrument for understanding personality differences – differences that can be the source of much misunderstanding and miscommunication between people. The MBTI can be effective in enabling you to identify your strengths and provides in a practical way a better understanding of yourself, your motivations, and potential areas for growth. Equally, it will also enable you to understand and appreciate those who differ from you.

(*Adapted from Wikipedia online*). The MBTI is a personality test designed to assist a person in identifying their personality preferences. Katherine Cook Briggs and her daughter Isobel Briggs Myers developed the test during World War II and its criteria follow from Carl Jung's theories in his work *Psychological Types*. The test is frequently used in the areas of pedagogy, group dynamics, employee training, leadership training etc. although scientific sceptics and academic psychologists have subjected it to considerable criticism in research literature.

Complete the following light-hearted questionnaire and establish what MBTI type you are.

Q1. Which is your most natural energy orientation?

Every person has two faces. One is directed towards the OUTER world of activities, excitements, people, and things. The other is directed inward to the INNER world of thoughts, interests, ideas, and imagination.

While these are two different but complementary sides of our nature, most people have an innate preference towards **energy** from the either the OUTER or INNER worlds. Thus one of their faces, either the *Extraverted* (E) or *Introverted* (I), takes the lead in their personality development and plays a more dominant role in their behavior.

Extraverted Characteristics	Introverted Characteristics
• Act first, think/reflect later	• Think/reflect first, then act
• Feel deprived when cut off from interaction with the outside world	• Regularly require an amount of "private time" to recharge batteries
• Usually open to and motivated by outside world of people and things	• Motivated internally, mind is sometimes so active it is "closed" to the outside world
• Enjoy wide variety and change in relationships with people	• Prefer one-to-one communication and relationships

Choose which best fits: ○ **Extraversion (E)**   ○ **Introversion (I)**

Q2. Which way of perceiving or understanding is most "automatic" or natural?

The **Sensing** (S) side of our brain notices the sights, sounds, smells and all the sensory details of the PRESENT. It categorizes, organizes, records and stores the specifics from the here and now. It is REALITY based.

The **Intuitive** (N) side of our brain seeks to understand, interpret and form OVERALL patterns of all the information that is collected and records these patterns and relationships. It speculates on POSSIBILITIES, including looking into and forecasting the FUTURE. It is imaginative and conceptual.

While both kinds of perceiving are necessary and used by all people, each of us instinctively tends to favor one over the other.

Sensing Characteristics	Intuitive Characteristics
• Mentally live in the Now, attending to present opportunities	• Mentally live in the Future, attending to future possibilities
• Using common sense and creating practical solutions is automatic-instinctual	• Using imagination and creating/inventing new possibilities is automatic-instinctual
• Memory recall is rich in detail of facts and past events	• Memory recall emphasizes patterns, contexts, and connections
• Best improvise from past experience	• Best improvise from theoretical understanding
• Like clear and concrete information; dislike guessing when facts are "fuzzy"	• Comfortable with ambiguous, fuzzy data and with guessing its meaning.

Choose which best fits: ○ Sensing (S)   ○ iNtuition (N)

Q3. Which way of forming Judgments and making choices is most natural?

The **Thinking** (T) side of our brain analyzes information in a DETACHED, objective fashion. It operates from factual principles, deduces and forms conclusions systematically. It is our logical nature.

The **Feeling** (F) side of our brain forms conclusions in an ATTACHED and somewhat global manner, based on likes/dislikes, impact on others, and human and aesthetic values. It is our subjective nature.

While everyone uses both means of forming conclusions, each person has a natural bias towards one over the other so that when they give us conflicting directions – one side is more dominant.

Thinking Characteristics	Feeling Characteristics
• Instinctively search for facts and logic in decision-making situations	• Instinctively employ personal feelings and impact on people in decision-making situations
• Naturally notices tasks and work to be accomplished.	• Naturally sensitive to people's needs and reactions
• Easily able to provide an objective and critical analysis	• Naturally seek consensus and popular opinions
• Accept conflict as a natural, normal part of relationships with people.	• Unsettled by conflict; have almost a toxic reaction to disharmony.

Choose which best fits: ○ Thinking (T)   ○ Feeling (F)

Q4. What is your action orientation towards the outside world?

All people use both *judging* (thinking and feeling) and *perceiving* (sensing and intuition) processes to store information, organize our thoughts, make decisions, take actions and manage our lives. Yet one of these processes (Judging **or** Perceiving) tends to take the lead in our relationship with the outside world while the other governs our inner world.

A **Judging** (J) style approaches the outside world WITH A PLAN and is oriented towards organizing one's surroundings, being prepared, making decisions and reaching closure and completion.

A **Perceiving** (P) style takes the outside world AS IT COMES and is adopting and adapting, flexible, open-ended and receptive to new opportunities and changing game plans.

Judging Characteristics	Perceiving Characteristics
• Plan many of the details in advance before moving into action.	• Comfortable moving into action without a plan; plan on-the-go.
• Focus on task-related action; complete meaningful segments before moving on.	• Like to multitask, have variety, mix work and play.
• Work best and avoid stress through keeping ahead of deadlines.	• Naturally tolerant of time pressure; work best close to deadlines.
• Naturally use targets, dates and standard routines to manage life.	• Instinctively avoid commitments which interfere with flexibility, freedom and variety

Choose which best fits: ○ **Judging (J)**   ○ **Perceiving (P)**

Working out your Myers Briggs type

The Myers Briggs model of personality is a theory of *preference*. Your Myers Briggs preferences are relatively static throughout life, however, your behaviour can change in different contexts.

A description of the Myers Briggs "letters"

The Myers Briggs model of personality is based on 4 preferences.

1. *Where, primarily, do you direct your energy?*

   If you prefer to direct your energy to deal with people, things, situations, or "the outer world", then your preference is for Extraversion. This is denoted by the letter "E".

   If you prefer to direct your energy to deal with ideas, information, explanations or beliefs, or "the inner world", then your preference is for Introversion. This is denoted by the letter "I".

2. ***How do you prefer to process information?***

If you prefer to deal with facts, what you know, to have clarity, or to describe what you see, then your preference is for Sensing. This is denoted by the letter "S".

If you prefer to deal with ideas, look into the unknown, to generate new possibilities or to anticipate what isn't obvious, then your preference is for Intuition. This is denoted by the letter "N".

3. ***How do you prefer to make decisions?***

If you prefer to decide on the basis of objective logic, using an analytical and detached approach, then your preference is for Thinking. This is denoted by the letter "T".

If you prefer to decide using values and/or personal beliefs, on the basis of what you believe is important or what you or others care about, then your preference is for Feeling. This is denoted by the letter "F".

4. ***How do you prefer to organise your life?***

If you prefer your life to be planned, stable and organised then your preference is for Judging (not to be confused with 'Judgemental', which is quite different). This is denoted by the letter "J".

If you prefer to go with the flow, to maintain flexibility and respond to things as they arise, then your preference is for Perception. This is denoted by the letter "P".

(adapted from ©www:personalpathways)

Now turn to the key on page 216 to see a snapshot view of what your type means.

As we all work with a wide variety of people, how can we best get on with the 8 types – especially when their personal preferences and ways of doing business may be very different from ours?

■ **Task 3**

What advice would you give someone working closely with:

a.   *an extravert e.g., set up teams, ...*
b.   *an introvert*
c.   *a sensor*
d.   *an intuitor*
e.   *a thinker*
f.   *a feeler*
g.   *a judger*
h.   *a perceiver*

17 Dealing with difficult people

The British, in particular, have made a fine art out of complaining and are the European champions. There is even a column devoted to moaning in the Times written by Jeremy Clarkson, the epitome of a grumpy old man. This chapter will help you deal assertively with some of the more impolite types you may come across.

■ Task 1

Read the extract from one of Jeremy Clarkson's articles and find words in the text which mean:

1. mild and pleasant
2. light rain
3. atomised
4. squirming
5. trepidation, apprehension
6. chilly
7. degree

My burning hate for patio heaters

The main reason I hate patio heaters is that they're trying to make Britain something it's not. In Australia you can eat and party outside because the climate is kind and the evenings are balmy. Whereas here, the climate is miserable and the evenings are freezing. This is great. In fact, it's precisely because we were brought up on a diet of drizzle and fish fingers that we had the biggest empire the world has ever seen.

Barbecues and patio heaters
Then there's the food itself, which, if you're outdoors, will have come from a barbecue. So, it will be nuked on one side and wriggling with salmonella on the other. And covered all over in a thin film of ash because at some point in the cooking process it will have fallen through the bars and into the charcoal.

Being invited to someone's house for a barbecue fills me with the same sort of horror and dread as being invited to someone's house for a fancy dress party. Especially if they have a patio heater, because then the guests end up like the food. Heated up on one side to the point where their flesh is starting to melt, and frozen solid on the other.

> *Greenpeace tells us that it's ridiculous to try and heat the outdoors and that if we get a bit nippy, we should wear a jumper. But as usual, I have a much better idea. Go inside and eat food that has been cooked in an oven. It'll taste better, you won't be eaten by a mosquito, you won't die of food poisoning, it's good for the economy and, if you turn the central heating up a notch or two and eat British tomatoes, you'll annoy Greenpeace even more than sheltering under a hot tin umbrella.*
>
> *Jeremy Clarkson*
> *Copyright 2006 Times Newspapers Ltd.*

■ Task 2

Find words/expressions in the text which the author uses to express negative feelings/opinions.

As mentioned before, the author is a typical out-and-out moaner and, what's more, seems to take pride in it. There are, of course, many different types of difficult people – let's look at some of them in more detail.

Dealing with different types of difficult people

For the sake of argument, difficult people have been divided into six categories. Obviously, there are many more sub-divisions we could make, but let's run with the most common types: the bulldozer, the sniper, the loose cannon, the 'yes-to-everything', the 'silent-as-a-tomb', and the out-and-out moaner.

■ Task 3

Have a look at the descriptions of a bulldozer and a sniper and insert the appropriate prepositions (in/out/of/from etc.) into the gaps. Some gaps may require more than one preposition.

The bulldozer

The bulldozer loves arguing and won't shut (1) ..... until they've had their say – so, let them run (2) ..... steam. Obviously, if they are taking too much airtime, then butt (3) ..... any way you can and don't worry too much (4) ..... being overly polite. But whatever you do, don't argue (5) ..... them or disagree overtly (6) ..... them. Maintain eye contact and state your opinions assertively. Keep the floor and don't let them drown you (7) ..... as they often tend to have very loud voices – (8) ..... all, don't let things descend (9) ..... an undignified slanging match however tempted you might feel.

The sniper

The sniper can be downright mean and sarcastic yet they often think they are being witty. This is the worst kind (10) ..... humour as it's always (11) ..... the expense (12) ..... someone else. Their favourite trick is to put others down (13) ..... public and they absolutely thrive (14) ..... taking a potshot (15) ..... every opportunity. To counter a sniper, you could paraphrase what they've said and ask them how and why their contribution is relevant (16) ..... the discussion (17) ..... hand as very often their comments are totally irrelevant and they're just doing what they're experts (18) ..... – sniping (19) ..... the sake (20) ..... it! If their comments are (21) ..... the matter (22) ..... hand, don't go along (23) ..... their negative viewpoints – ask others what their opinions are and try to reach consensus. (24) ..... this way, you will take the wind (25) ..... the sniper's sails.

■ Task 4

Have a look at the descriptions of a loose cannon and a 'yes-to-everything' and insert the article: zero article – /a/an/the into the gaps. Please see Appendix D on page 164 for an overview of article usage.

The loose cannon

(1) ..... loose cannon is very unpredictable, liable to explode for no (2) ..... good reason, and very embarrassing to be around – they thrive on throwing tantrums much like (3) ..... toddler who freaks out when they are forbidden to do something. Once they've gone ballistic, give them time to regain control of themselves but if this doesn't seem to be happening, then stop them any way you can – even if it means shouting "Stop!" You need to show them that you take their concerns seriously but, (4) ..... first and foremost, you need to bring (5) ..... temperature down for (6) ..... sake of (7) ..... whole group. If you can and you think it might help, have some one-on-one time with (8) ..... loose cannon and try to find out what sets them off.

The 'yes-to-everything'

The 'yes-to-everything' needs to be liked – they always try to please everyone and offend no one. So they say "yes" to anything and everything but have absolutely no intention of following through. Or they'll say "yes" to so many things that they'd have to work (9) ..... 24/7 to get everything done. One way of dealing with them is to let them know you value them and to listen carefully to what they say – there could be (10) ..... hidden messages beneath all that good humour. If you need them to fulfil (11) ..... task, give them very structured assignments with (12) ..... clear and doable deadline.

■ **Task 5**

Read the descriptions of the 'silent-as-a-tomb' and the 'out-and-out moaner' and make a note of what strategies you could use to deal with them.

Example

▶ don't encourage the out-and-out moaner to continue to complain by asking them detailed questions about every aspect of their complaint.

The 'silent-as-a-tomb'

The silent-as-a-tomb is just that – they don't express their opinions openly and let you think that they agree with everything, when in fact they often don't. A typical saying of theirs is "I told you so" when something doesn't go according to plan – but, of course, they didn't because they never opened their mouths in the first place.

The out-and-out moaner

The out-and-out moaner hasn't heard of looking on the bright side – they're permanently on the dark side. Life is a pain for them and they are perpetually disappointed and always complaining loudly about it. They also tend to be nit-pickers and have no problem finding fault with everything. The out-and-out moaner has a Dracula-like effect on groups – they suck the lifeblood out of discussions and dampen enthusiasm in group dynamics.

■ **Task 6**

Read through the six categories again and think about whether you know anyone who fits one of these descriptions.

Positive vs negative communication

It goes without saying that difficult people tend to use negative language but as these people can make us feel utterly miserable, defensive, and stressed out, we too can fall very easily into the trap of using negative language. Remember negative communication is: non-communication, destructive, never brings closure, and never achieves victory. Think about the connotations of a person in the public eye using 'No comment' when asked for their opinion on a matter. The effect that this utterance has is to alienate us from the speaker, we immediately think that they are guilty of whatever they're refusing to comment on, and we start to imagine that they may have done something even worse. Newspapers all over the world, of course, go to town whenever there's a 'no comment' response to their reporters' questions. By contrast, have a look at an excerpt from Martin Luther King's famous speech. He said:

I have a dream that one day this nation will rise up and live out the true meaning of its creed: "We hold these truths to be self-evident: that all men are created equal." ... I have a dream that my four children will one day live in a nation where they will not be judged by the color of their skin but by the content of their character. I have a dream today.

Copyright: Martin Luther King, August 28, 1963.
From a speech delivered on the steps of the Lincoln Memorial in Washington DC

He did not say, "My dream will not come true and, therefore, it's not worth having. My children will never cease to be the targets of racism – they'll always be victims because of the colour of their skin and so I have no dream." A truly powerful communicator will always use positive rather than negative communication to drive their point home.

■ Task 7

Have a look at these examples of negative communication and find another way of getting the message across in a more positive manner. For example: these figures are really bad – these figures could be better

1. *That's not how it's done*
2. *You're wrong*
3. *It won't work*
4. *I see no reason to disagree*
5. *I don't like X*
6. *Just because I didn't say X, it doesn't mean ...*
7. *That's not a bad idea*
8. *There is no real reason for us not to cooperate*
9. *We can't do it without you*
10. *There isn't any right way to do X*

Assertiveness

In general, we need to be assertive in our communication style and especially when we're dealing with difficult people. Think about when you're asked to do something that you don't really want to do and, also, don't have the time to do, what do you say? "Yes, of course I will", "You must be joking!", or "I'd really like to help you but I'm afraid I haven't got the time?"

These responses are examples of 3 common approaches to asserting your needs. 'Non-assertive' behaviour happens if you express your needs as being less important than other people's; 'aggressive' behaviour is when you express your needs as being more important than others', 'assertive' behaviour stems from the belief that your needs are as important as those of other people and should be the target behaviour for PAs and secretaries working both on a national and international basis. Assertive behaviour involves:

▶ standing up for your rights without treading on other people

▶ expressing your feelings and opinions in a suitable and appropriate manner

▶ showing you are listening to and understand other people's opinions and feelings

The problem is how to be assertive in a sensitive way. Imagine this situation: Maria and Susanna both work as PAs to the CEO of a large company and share the same boss. Whenever, there is a challenging task, the boss assigns it to Maria and continues to assign the more routine tasks to Susanna. The boss has never indicated that he finds Maria more competent than Susanna. Unsurprisingly, Susanna is hurt and frustrated by her boss' behaviour and decides to do something about it.

■ Task 8

Look at the three ways Susanna handles the situation and a) decide in each case whether her behaviour is aggressive, non-assertive, or assertive and b) analyse the effectiveness of her response and the likely outcome.

1. Susanna knocks quietly at the boss' door and sidles in and starts to speak, whilst looking at the floor. "Er, er, sorry to bother you but I was just kind of thinking about the work I do. It's really not important if you haven't got the time but what I really wanted to say was that I'm very happy here but mm mm what I mean is ... (pause) ... the job er er ..."

2. Susanna marches into her boss' office and stands right in front of his desk, staring him right in the face and yells, "Why the hell do I always get the boring jobs? You always give Maria the interesting stuff and I get the rubbish! I'm just as good as she is and unless you change this, I'm out of here!"

3. Susanna arranges a meeting with her boss. At the meeting she says, "I don't know whether you've realised this but over the last few weeks, you've given all the interesting jobs to Maria. As far as I know, you think we're both equally competent yet I continue to get the routine tasks. I feel rather hurt by this and I'd like to have the opportunity to take on some more challenging tasks too. How can we remedy the situation?"

The following points will help you to distinguish appropriate language linked to being 'assertive' from being 'non-assertive' or 'aggressive.'

Non-assertive

▶ avoidance of 'I'

▶ qualifying phrases e.g., *'it's only my opinion ...'*, 'sorry to bother you ...', 'I wonder if ...'

▶ using a lot of fillers, such as: *'you know'*, *'sort of'*, *'like'* etc.

▶ putting yourselves down e.g., *'I'm not very good at this ...'*, *'I know I'm not an expert'*

▶ using phrases which make it easy for others to ignore your needs e.g., *'it's not really important'*, *'it doesn't matter'* etc.

▶ using long convoluted sentences often justifying yourself

Aggressive

▶ overuse of *'I'*

▶ stating your opinions as facts e.g., *'that strategy won't work'*, *'that's a bad idea'*

▶ using threatening phrases, e.g., *'you'd better..'*

▶ putting others down or belittling their contributions *'you must be joking'*, *'you can't be serious'* etc.

▶ overuse of strong modals e.g., *'you have to'* *'you must..'* etc.

▶ blaming others e.g., *'it was your fault'*, *'it was your idea'* *'you decided to ...'* etc.

Assertive

▶ making contributions that are brief and to the point

▶ Using open-ended questions to elicit contributions from others, e.g.,: *'What do you think?'*, *'How do you feel about such an approach?'*

▶ using *'I'* statements where appropriate e.g., *'I think ...'*, *'I feel ...'*, *'I'd like ...'*

▶ distinguishing clearly between fact and experience e.g., *'in my opinion ...'*, *'in my experience ...'*

▶ avoiding strong modals e.g., *'You could ...'*, *'It would be better if you ...'*, *'I think you should'*

▶ actively looking for cooperative solutions to problems, e.g., *'how can we solve this?'*

Being assertive

■ Task 9

Have a look at the following situations and decide what you would say. Your objective is to be assertive.

1.   *You are working on a very important project at the moment together with a colleague. But whenever you ask your colleague to do something on the project, she's always too busy. You are becoming increasingly frustrated. Send her an email explaining how you feel and asking her if you can meet her to talk about it.*

2.   *One of your team members left you a message asking you to take on some extra work. You are very busy at the moment and already spending long hours in the office and, therefore, don't want to add even more to your heavy workload. Leave her a voicemail refusing to take on the work and explaining why.*

3.   *You have enrolled on a two-day course on PowerPoint presentations – the course starts tomorrow and you made the arrangements two months ago. Your boss, who is currently away on business, has just left you a voicemail asking you to cancel the course as she needs you to prepare a presentation on a new product your company is launching. Send her an email explaining that you really need to attend the course to improve your PowerPoint skills and pointing out that a) the graphics department could prepare the slides and b) that if you go on the course, you will be able to prepare more professional slides in the future.*

One aspect of being assertive is choice of language but assertiveness also has certain characteristics:

Owning feelings e.g., "it hurts my feelings"	Maintain eye contact and appropriate body language – don't look at the floor, hunch over etc.
Avoiding confrontation – don't use threats, evaluations, or dogmatic terms	Maintain a firm and pleasant tone of voice – don't yell or mumble
Use specific statements directed to the situation, "as far as I know, you think we're equally competent."	Avoid 'um' and 'er' – it makes you sound indecisive

N.B. *Cultural differences*
Remember that assertive behaviour is primarily practised in Anglo-Saxon/North European cultures. In Far Eastern cultures, 'saving face' can be more important than achieving personal satisfaction. However, in Latin cultures, self-expression may go far beyond what we find acceptable to the point of 'machismo' especially when applied to men. Thus, how we use assertiveness may be perceived by other cultures as too aggressive or, on the other hand, as not assertive enough.

A rule of thumb is to use your common sense. If you are communicating with people from a different culture, observe their behaviour and then decide how assertive you need to be.

Tact and Diplomacy

Tact and diplomacy are closely interlinked both with dealing with difficult people and with being assertive. The English language lends itself to being tactful and diplomatic and speakers of English are generally far less direct than speakers of other languages e.g., speakers of German. How do we do this? We achieve this through not only our tone of voice but also through our choice of language. Here are some ways in which we make our utterances more diplomatic.

Making language more diplomatic

1. Use *would*, *could* or *might* to make what you say more tentative:

That is too long a delay	– That would be too long a delay
That does not meet our specifications	– That might not meet our specifications
You must visit our London office	– You could visit our London office

2. **Questions** rather than statements make your views less dogmatic:

It's a good idea to check with head office first?	– Is it a good idea to check with head office first?
The risk involved in this is far too serious	– Would the risk be too serious?
He's not the right person for the job	– Is he the right person for the job?

3. Introductory **'softening'** phrases prepare your listeners for an unwelcome or unhelpful message:

I'm afraid ...	Frankly ...
With respect ...	To be honest ...
To put it bluntly ...	If I may say so ...

> **Example**
>
> A: Could I speak to John, please?
> B: I'm afraid he's out of the office.

4. Use **qualifying** words to soften what you say:

a slight misunderstanding   a bit of a problem
some reservations   a short delay

5. Soften your message by using a comparative form:

Would Tuesday be a better day to meet?
Would the afternoon be more convenient?
Option C might be more cost-effective.

■ Task 10

What would you write instead? Rewrite these sentences in a more tactful and diplomatic style suitable to business correspondence.

1. *My report is going to be late.*
2. *I am not willing to give you more time to complete the project.*
3. *You still owe us EUR 5,000.*
4. *This information is wrong.*
5. *We want an immediate answer to this email.*
6. *I cannot accept your invitation because I'm already busy that day.*
7. *We can't give you the information because we don't know.*
8. *Can you let us know the minute you've sent the brochure?*

■ Task 11

Change the tone of this email to make it both more diplomatic and more formal.

Dear Mr Oldman

We are changing the date of the meeting from Tuesday 2nd August to Thursday 4th August. This is because the new chairman wants to meet you and he is only free on that day. So ignore the fax I sent you yesterday telling you the meeting was on Tuesday. I know you're actually going on holiday on Thursday but you'll just have to put it off. Sorry about that.

Frances Alerma

Appendix A Linking Words – A Summary

Sequencing	Addition	Purpose	Reason
first(ly) (I) second(ly) (I) finally (I) lastly (I) then (I) next (I) after that (I) afterwards (I)	furthermore (I/M) also (M) too (F) moreover I/M) in addition (I) besides (/M) what is more (I) not to mention the fact that (M) not only ... but also (I/M)	so that (M) in order to (I/M) so as to (I/M) in case (I/M) with the purpose/ intention of (M)	because (I/M) since/as (I/M) owing to/due to (the fact that) (I/M) on the grounds that (I/M) in view of (I/M) for this reason (I/M) otherwise (M)
Exemplification	**Clarification**	**Contrast**	**Similarity**
for example (I/M) for instance (I/M) e.g., (M) such as (M)	namely (M) i.e., (M) after all (inf.) in other words (I) in fact (I/M)	in spite of (the fact that) (I/M) while (I/M) in contrast (I) on the one hand ... on the other hand (I/M) but (I/M) on the contrary (I/M) although (I/M) whereas (I/M)	similarly (I/M) in the same way (I/M)
Result	**Time**		
consequently (I/M) otherwise (M) therefore (I/M) so (inf.) (I/M) thus (very formal) (I/M) if not (I/M) as a result/ consequence (I)	at first (I/M) at last (I/M) meanwhile (M) previously (I/M)		

I = word/phrase usually in the initial position in a sentence
M = word/phrase usually in the mid position in a sentence
F = word/phrase usually in the final position in a sentence
Inf = informal usage

Appendix B Punctuation

Punctuation in written English is used as a means of conveying your message clearly and unambiguously.

The **full stop** has two main uses:

▶ To signify the end of a sentence, e.g., *The European Union has faced a lot of opposition from some political parties in all countries. There is still a long way to go before Europe is truly united.*

▶ To show that a word has been abbreviated, e.g., *Mr., Dr.,* e.g.,

Remember to keep sentences in English short and simple otherwise it may be difficult for your reader to follow you.

The **comma** is used in sentences to show a pause between sense groups of words, e.g., *The car industry expanded in the eighties, slowed down in the nineties, and it is anybody's guess what it will do in the coming decade.*

The comma is also used to separate words in a list, e.g., *The steel, coal, chemical, and gas industries all face a lot of competition from the Far East.*

Commas are also used for non-defining relative clauses, e.g., *The response, which came rather late, surprised everyone concerned.* Remember that in defining relative clauses no commas are needed e.g., *The item which you ordered is no longer in production.*

Commas are not generally used before linking words like *or, but* or *then,* e.g., *The presentation was quite long but everyone listened with great concentration.* Commas are, however, used after subclauses in front position, e.g., *Although interest rates have been falling, there is no sign of any recovery in the economy.*

The **semi-colon** is not used as much nowadays as it used to be. It is mainly used to separate main clauses whose ideas are closely linked, e.g., *The advertising campaign was extremely successful; it helped us to sell more products than our competitors.* However, the above sentence could be rewritten using *so ... ... that* or *moreover.*

The **colon** is normally used to introduce an example or a quotation or a list, e.g., *The following brands are the best selling soft drinks in the UK: Coca-Cola, Pepsi-Cola etc.*

Brackets are used:

▶ To separate an additional idea from the rest of the sentence, e.g., *A shortcut (although this is not recommended for beginners) could be to work on both programmes at once.*

▶ To give a reference source, e.g., *The results obtained (Appendix A) demonstrated a regional difference.*

Question marks are used:

▶ At the end of direct questions, e.g., *Where are you going?*

▶ At the end of rhetorical questions, e.g., *And I ask myself, who needs this kind of problem anyway?*

Remember that indirect questions don't have question marks, e.g., *She asked me where the station was.*

The **hyphen** is used to link together words or parts of words which start at the end of one line and finish on the next. Remember that when you separate a word from one line to the next, you should never divide a syllable. A sensible rule is that if you don't know how to split a word or you're not sure, then **don't do it.**

The **apostrophe** has two main uses:

▶ To show that a letter has been missed out in contractions, e.g., *it's, won't, can't, needn't* etc.

▶ To show possession, e.g., *The manager's office*

The apostrophe is probably the most frequently misused piece of punctuation in the English language. People most commonly misuse it when they want to make a word plural, e.g.,

Grow your own potatoe's.
Back in the 1990's ...
All the department's were represented.

All these examples are wrong, for a very good reason – you don't need an apostrophe anywhere to pluralise a word. That isn't what apostrophes were invented for.

The possessive

Add an 's' to the person, people or thing doing the possessing: the children's shoes, the tree's shade, the cat's eyes. The apostrophe goes after whoever is possessing, so in the last example, if you were talking about the eyes of lots of cats the apostrophe would go after the final 's' of cats: the cats' eyes.

▶ A good way to remember it is to say to yourself 'the ... *belonging to* the ...'
▶ If they're the eyes belonging to the cat (singular) you would write: the cat's eyes.

If they're the eyes belonging to the cats (plural) you would write: the cats' eyes.

If the person or people (or cats) doing the possessing already have an 's' on the end, you don't add another one; simply stick the apostrophe on the end – that's why you've never seen anyone write 'the cats's eyes'. The only times when you would add an 's' after a singular word that ends in 's' are:

▶ If it's a proper name (Mr Jones's, St James's)
▶ If the word ends in a double 'ss' (the boss's).

You never use an apostrophe with a possessive pronoun (a word indicating possession which replaces a noun). These are words like: yours, hers, its, theirs, ours.

It's and its

A lot of people find these two words very confusing; 'its' is a possessive pronoun and therefore has no apostrophe, while 'it's' is short for 'it is' and does have one. The easiest way to tell each time you write the word is to say it in your head as 'it is'. If it makes sense, it's short for it is and has an apostrophe. Otherwise it doesn't. For example, 'I gave the dog its breakfast'. Try the technique: 'I gave the dog it is breakfast.' Complete nonsense. It clearly isn't short for it is, so it shouldn't have an apostrophe. Here's another example: 'It's a great day to go swimming'. Try the technique: 'It is a great day to go swimming'. That makes sense – it's short for 'it is' so it *does* have an apostrophe, in place of the missing 'i.'

Appendix C Proofreader's marks

The following marks are standard proofreading marks. Only the most commonly used have been included. Depending on the content of your text, you may need to use other symbols, e.g., superscript and subscript for formulas.

A professional proofreader puts a mark in the line and writes the correction in the margin. An editor makes corrections within the line rather than in the margin (in part because an editor's changes are typically more extensive), which is why editors prefer to work with double-spaced copy.

Symbol	Meaning	Example
ℐ or ♂ or ⁊	delete	take it out
◯	close up	print as o ne word
ℬ	delete and close up	clo͜se up
∧ or › or ⋏	caret	insert here ⌐something
#	insert a space	put one here
eq#	space evenly	space evenly where indicated
stet	let stand	let marked text stand as set
tr	transpose	change order the
/	used to separate two or more marks and often as a concluding stroke at the end of an insertion	
⌐	set farther to the left	⌐ too far to the right
⌐	set farther to the right	too⌐ far to the left
⌒	set as ligature (such as æ)	encyclopaedia
⸗	align horizontally	alignment

Symbol	Meaning	Example
‖	align vertically	‖ align with surrounding text
✗	broken character	imperfect
▯	indent or insert em quad space	
¶	begin a new paragraph	
ⓢⓟ	spell out	set ⟨5 lbs.⟩ as five pounds
cap	set in CAPITALS	set nato as NATO
sm cap or s.c.	set in SMALL CAPITALS	set signal as SIGNAL
lc	set in lowercase	set South as south
ital	set in *italic*	set oeuvre as *oeuvre*
rom	set in roman	set *mensch* as mensch
bf	set in **boldface**	set important as **important**
= or -/ or ⌢ or /=/	hyphen	multi-colored
⅟N or en or /N/	en dash	1965–72
⅟M or em or /M/	em (or long) dash	Now — at last! — we know.
⌄	superscript or superior	²as in πr^2
⌃	subscript or inferior	₂ as in H_2O
◇ or ⋎	centered	◇ for a centered dot in $p \cdot q$
↱	comma	
↓	apostrophe	
⊙	period	
; or ;/	semicolon	

Symbol	Meaning	Example
⁚ or ⊕	colon	
⸂⸃ or ⸜⸝	quotation marks	
(/)	parentheses	
[/]	brackets	
OK/?	query to author: has this been set as intended?	

Appendix D   The use of the articles a/an/the/ zero (no) article

A countable noun is the name of something that can be counted: one book, two books etc. A non-countable noun is the name of something that cannot be counted: milk, money, freedom, justice. A non-countable noun does not take "a" or "an" and does not have a plural form.

	Use "a" or "an"	Use "the"	Don't Use "a," "an," or "the"
General Rules	Use "a" or "an" with a singular countable noun when you mean "one of many". • Annie is a student (one of many students).	Use "the" with any noun when the meaning is specific; for example, when the noun names the only one (or one) of a kind. • Adam was the first man (the only 'first man'). • London is the capital of the UK (only one city can be 'the capital').	Don't use "a," "an," or "the" with a non-countable noun when you mean "in general." • Coffee has gone up in price.
	Use "a" or "an" the first time you use a noun in a paragraph • I saw a great film last night.	Use "the" the second time you use that same noun in the same paragraph • The film I saw was about ...	Don't use "a," "an," or "the" with a plural countable noun when you mean "in general." • Classical music concerts are very relaxing (in general).
Title	Use "a" or "an" if the title is not a specific title. • a nurse • a doctor • a princess	Use "the" if only one person has the title. • the President of the US • the Queen of England	Don't use "a," "an," or "the" if the person's name is given. • President Bush • Queen Elizabeth

	Use "a" or "an"	Use "the"	Don't Use "a," "an," or "the"
Names of Countries	Non-specific • a country	Use "the" if the name of the country is plural or indicates a group (of states, islands, etc.) • the United States • the Netherlands • the United Kingdom	Don't use "a," "an," or "the" for other countries, e.g., • Russia • South Africa • Holland • Canada • England
Names of Continents	Non-specific • a continent		Don't use "a," "an," or "the" before the names of continents • Asia • Europe • Australia
Names of Some Geographical Areas		Use "the" • the South Pole • the South • the Middle East	Don't use "a," "an," or "the" • Western Europe
Names of Cities and States	Non-specific • a city • a state	• the Hague	Don't use "a," "an," or "the" • London • Paris • Beijing
Names of Streets		• the High Street • the Champs Elysées	Don't use "a," "an," or "the" • Belgrave Street • Fifth Avenue
Names of Oceans, Rivers, Seas, Deserts, Forests, Canals	Use a/an for non-specific • an ocean • a canal • a sea • a desert	Use "the" • the Indian Ocean • the North Sea • the Suez Canal • the Sahara	

	Use "a" or "an"	Use "the"	Don't Use "a," "an," or "the"
Names of Lakes	Non-specific • a lake		Don't use "a," "an," or "the" • Lake Michigan • Lake Geneva

Appendix E   Conditional forms in the English language

Sample sentences

Zero conditional
If the studio light is red, they're recording.

First conditional
If the job is not completed within three months, a penalty clause will come into effect.

Second conditional
If we had more time, it would be a lot easier.

Third conditional
If you had paid earlier, you wouldn't have paid interest on the debt.

Mixed conditional (third + second)
If he had let us know about his difficulties earlier, he wouldn't be in this situation now.

Grammatical structure

Type of conditional	If clause	Main clause
Zero conditional	If + present tense	present tense
Example	If we have it in writing,	it's legally binding.
First conditional	If + present tense	future form
Example	If we meet this deadline,	we'll get further business from this client.
Second conditional	If + past simple/continuous tense	would/could/should/ought to/must + infinitive
Example	If we had more people working on it,	we could get it finished by the 5th.
Third conditional	If + past perfect	would/could/should/ought to/must+ have + past participle
Example	If we'd sent the reminder earlier,	we could have avoided this problem.

Type of conditional	If clause	Main clause
Mixed conditional (third + second) Example	If + past perfect If we'd checked the proofs more carefully,	would/could/should/ought to/must + infinitive there wouldn't be so many mistakes in the article.
Polite phrase using a conditional form in the if clause Example	If + would + infinitive If you would like to take a seat,	future form I'll tell Mr. Blanco you're here.

1 Communicating with clarity KEY

■ Task 1

1. NS – the sentence makes no sense because you cannot use lubrication oil (engine oil) for cooking purposes

2. S

3. NS – there is no main verb

4. NS – there is no subject

5. S

6. S

7. S

8. NS – there is no subject and no main verb – the expression is just hanging in thin air

9. NS – there is no main verb

10. S

■ Task 2 Suggested answer

In the US, teachers need to publish before they are promoted.

■ Task 3 Suggested answer

There are three reasons why exercise is good for you. First, it keeps you fit and can help to keep your weight down. Second, it keeps you healthy and can reduce the likelihood of having heart problems. Finally, it can help to keep stress levels down and has been known to relieve depression. In conclusion, everyone should do some form of regular exercise.

■ Task 4

1. Although/While

2. Firstly

3. Consequently

4. also

5. In contrast

6. so/therefore

7. Secondly

8. furthermore

9. therefore

10. otherwise

11. For example

12. thus

13. also

14. Finally

15. moreover

16. Meanwhile

■ Task 5 Suggested answers

1. Hello this is ...., PA to Mr X. I am afraid that Mr X has been held up in Italy and will therefore not be able to make the meeting at 9 tomorrow. He suggests meeting on Friday afternoon at a time convenient for you or if Friday doesn't suit you, perhaps you could meet him next Tuesday. My telephone number is .... Maybe you could give me a ring and let me know what day and time would be suitable for you. Thank you.

2. Hello this is ...., PA to Mr X. He has asked me to call you to arrange a telephone conference with Mr Wang. My phone number is .... Could you please give me a ring and let me know at what time and on what day would be the best for Mr X to call Mr Wang. I look forward to hearing from you. Thank you.

■ Task 6 Suggested answer

Hello could I speak to Ana Ribero please. It's ....' PA to Mr Braun.

Ana, how are you? How are things in Madrid? I hope the weather's better there than here. I am ringing about the meeting in Rome. We know that it's not a very convenient place for you to get to but we're planning to rotate the monthly meetings from now on so that we can all get to know the other subsidiaries. We'd very much appreciate it if you could join us for the meeting. Your input is always valued. In fact, we'd very much like to have the next meeting in Madrid and would welcome your recommendations on arranging accommodation. If you need any help with your travel arrangements, please feel free to contact me – I'd be delighted to assist you.

■ **Task 7 Suggested answer**

To: Mr X
From: Karl Braun
Subject: European Marketing Meeting

Following my email sent yesterday, we're sorry to inform you that the venue of the next meeting has been changed from Rome to Oslo. This change in plan is due to the fact that Clara Sullivan, our Marketing Director (US), has another meeting in Oslo on the same day and we feel it is important for her to be with us on this occasion.

I appreciate that this will involve changing your plans but, in the circumstances, we feel there is no option. Would you kindly let us have any special requests regarding the agenda? My PA will call you in a few days to discuss this further, and I am sure we can have a very useful meeting on this occasion in Oslo.

Please remember that if there's any help we can give you with travel arrangements, we would be delighted to do so.

Once again, our apologies for causing you any inconvenience.

Regards

Karl

---

2 Best-practice emails and working in multi-cultural teams KEY

■ Task 1 Answers

1. B
2. D
3. C
4. A

■ Task 2

1. flaming; unfriendly tone; no greeting; no closing
2. no greeting
3. no greeting; too many abbreviations/acronyms
4. no greeting; general lack of clarity; generally inappropriate content
A. no greeting; unfriendly tone
B. flaming; unfriendly tone; no greeting; no closing
C. no greeting; no closing; use of abbreviations; unfriendly tone
D. general lack of clarity; difficult to read; no greeting; no closing

■ Task 3 Suggested answers

1. We have a problem with Makro due to late delivery.
2. The meeting is on Tuesday next week at 11 a.m. in the Green Room and all are expected to attend.
3. The alarms will be tested every Monday at 8 a.m.
4. Please don't forget to bring the presentation on team building.
A. I am bringing the presentation.
B. I have solved the problem.
C. Thank you for the information.
D. Is it absolutely essential for me to attend the meeting?

■ Task 4

1. No
2. Yes
3. Yes
4. Yes but write the agenda first, attach it to the email, and apologise
5. No
6. No. It would be better to do it face-to-face.

■ **Task 5 Suggested answer**

Dear Mr/Ms X

We had a visitor to our company, XYZ Ltd, staying at your hotel this week for three days. We were most dissatisfied with the service you provided.

Firstly, the toilet didn't function for two out of the three days that he stayed with you – we find this completely unacceptable.

Secondly, you had informed us that all rooms had Internet access but, in the room in question, Mr X was unable to connect to the Internet which seriously inconvenienced him.

Thirdly, when he ordered room service, he had to wait for an unacceptable length of time for it to arrive and when it did finally arrive the food was so cold it was inedible.

You will of course understand our reluctance to settle the bill in the light of these complaints. We look forward to hearing from you and are sure that we can come to a mutually acceptable agreement.

Yours sincerely

. . . .

■ **Task 6**

1. draw on
2. diversity
3. issues
4. servicing
5. misunderstandings
6. understatement
7. to bring to the surface
8. expectations
9. vital
10. ever-flowing

■ **Task 7 Suggested answers**

1. Because the British tend to use understatement and may not signal their problems directly.

2. Through being open and honest about what you expect the outcome of a communication to be, whether it's a phone call or an email, and also about which type of communication you would prefer to receive if you are signalling that you

have a problem. It's always good to talk about what you expect and want from colleagues.

3. Because there is more person-to-person contact; it is an interactive method of communication; you can very often hear how a person feels from what they say or don't say etc.; you can guess the person's reaction from the tone of their voice.

■ Task 8 Suggested answers

CL: Hello, this is Clementine Liu from the Shanghai office. How are you?

1. You: Hello Clementine. I'm fine thank you and how are you?

CL: I'm fine too thank you and how's the weather?

2. You: Raining I'm afraid. What about over there?

CL: It's quite humid here but luckily we have air conditioning. How was your holiday?

3. You: It was great – really relaxing but not long enough. You know how it is – the first week you need to relax and then just when you're starting to feel better it's time to come home again. Still, I'm feeling refreshed.

CL: Oh good! It's very nice to talk to you again. I was just wondering if you got my voicemail?

4. You: Yes, I did and I was wondering what exactly I can do to help you.

CL: I've got a bit of a problem as I said. Do you think you would have the time to just check my charts for me?

5. You: I can make the time. If it's just checking a few charts, I'd be happy to help you.

CL: That would be great. Thank you so much, I'll email them through to you and I'm really looking forward to seeing you again.

6. You: You're welcome and I'm looking forward to seeing you too.

CL: Thank you once again and goodbye.

■ Task 9 Suggested answer

Hi, this is ...., calling from .... How are you? I'm returning your call about Mr A and that he wants to reschedule the meeting. I'm sorry but it's going to be a bit difficult because it's rather late for so many people to reorganise their schedule. How about if we rescheduled the start of the meeting to 9 and pushed lunch till 12.30. That would suit everyone. Please let me know what you think and if there's anything else I can do, I'd be happy to help.

3 Building business relationships KEY

■ Task 1

1. interlocutor
2. facilitates
3. to get straight down to
4. achieve
5. fosters
6. pingpongs
7. to broaden
8. dismissive
9. engaged in
10. tool

■ Task 2

1. b
2. c
3. a
4. a
5. b
6. c

■ Task 3 Suggested answer

Yes, I have actually. I went there last year and stayed right in the centre of town. I specifically went to London to see the Edward Hopper exhibition at the Tate Modern.

I really liked the Tate Modern and the Millennium Bridge and all the great restaurants in the Docklands. London really has a lot of energy and I always feel good when I go there.

■ Task 4

1. S
2. R
3. R
4. S
5. S
6. R
7. R

8. S but it's not always appropriate to start with something negative.
9. R
10. R

■ Task 5 Suggested answers

1. Good morning, I'm .... from .... How do you do?

2. It's nice to meet you

3. Would you like a cup of coffee? I hope you had a good journey and that you found the office easily. Is this your first visit to ....? What do you think of it so far? You really must visit ....

■ Task 6 Suggested answers

▶ I'd really like to know more about what you do.
▶ Tell me about your work.
▶ How do you do X?
▶ How did you achieve Y?
▶ What made you come to the seminar?
▶ What takeaways do you hope to get?
▶ Why did you choose this particular workshop?

■ Task 7 Suggested answers

1. Oh dear!
2. That's great!
3. I follow you.
4. That's terrible!
5. I'm with you.
6. Oh, no!
7. Good!
8. What a shame!
9. I'm so sorry.
10. Oh, dear!

■ Task 8 Suggested answers

1. Would you like me to send it for you?
2. I can call the credit card companies and the police for you, if you'd like me to.
3. Shall I phone our taxi company for you?

■ Task 9 Suggested answers

1. May I take your coat?
2. Can I get you a cup of coffee?

3. Shall I show you where the ladies/gents is?
4. Would you like me to get you a hairdryer?

■ Task 10 Suggested answer

From: ....
To: Pamela Hutchinson
Subject: Last week's conference
Dear Pamela, It was so nice to meet you that I thought I'd send you an email. I really enjoyed talking to you and it would be great if we could keep in touch. You said you were coming to Germany soon. Let me know when as it'd be good to meet up again. Look forward to hearing from you soon. Best regards ....

■ Task 11 Suggested answer

From: ....
To: Pamela Hutchinson
Subject: re coming to Germany
Dear Pam That's great news and I will be around during that time. From my side, Oct 18 is probably the best for me as I still have a lot of work at the moment and also for the next couple of months. How about if we meet at your hotel at 7 and go and have a drink by the river and then go and have a bite to eat in the old town? There are some really nice restaurants there that don't cost an arm and a leg and have a really good atmosphere. Let me know what you think. Best regards ....

4 Delegating KEY

■ **Task 1**

1. D
2. I
3. B
4. G
5. J
6. M
7. K
8. E
9. L
10. A
11. F
12. H
13. C

■ **Task 2**

1. N
2. A
3. N
4. A/N
5. N
6. N
7. A
8. A
9. A
10. N

■ **Task 3   Suggested answers**

1. Eva, I need you to redraft the contract by the end of the day.

2. It would be great if you could meet the visitors when they arrive tonight, Mark.

3. Carla, would you be able to take on the organising of the Geneva conference?

4. Now, what I want you to do Tom is contact everyone going to the 2pm meeting and tell them it's now going to be in room 108.

5. Emma, do you think you could help me out by collating the folders for the seminar? I seem to be running out of time here.

■ **Task 4**

A. 7
B. 4
C. 1
D. 8
E. 2
F. 6
G. 3
H. 5

■ **Task 5**

These are very much suggested answers. The order in which a conference is organised will depend on the size and nature of the event.

5. Decide on promotion
10. Order flowers
12. Run through the day and check all details
2. Calculate an effective budget
9. Order catering
7. Define layout and seating of venue
4. Develop the programme
11. Contingency plans for bad weather/latecomers etc.
6. Order conference material/presentation kits
1. Define the aims and target audience
8. List equipment needed
3. Select date and venue

■ **Task 6**

Check Appendix A for alternative words/phrases for each category, e.g., purpose.

1. result e.g., as a result
2. purpose e.g., in order to
3. reason e.g., because
4. result e.g., consequently/ addition e.g., in addition
5. result e.g., therefore
6. addition e.g., also
7. reason e.g., otherwise
8. sequencing e.g., Finally,/In addition e.g., Furthermore
9. purpose e.g., so that

■ **Task 7   Suggested answers**

Budgeting plays a vital role./ An effective budget/ is crucial/ to the success of the conference./ Work out your costs./ How much is needed for fixed costs,/ for example,/

the venue hire,/ speakers fees/ and so on./ Then/ calculate the amount needed for variable costs/ such as additional hotel accommodation,/ extra delegates' packs/ etc./Again,/ check your figures with the venue staff/ and ask for their input./ And/ always allow/ a contingency of at least 10%/ to cover unforeseen expenses./

If the conference is to be attended by delegates/ from overseas offices/ or by delegates/ who are not employees of the company,/ it needs to be promoted/ through news releases./ The Internet is a good resource./ Advertisements in specialist magazines and journals/ need to be placed/ well in advance./ Mail shots of publicity literature/ can be sent to likely participants./ Although the draft programme may include the phrase/ *speaker to be announced,*/ it is crucial/ to secure top-quality speakers early/ to ensure a successful promotion campaign./ A central system must be set up/ to receive and track replies,/ handle bookings/ and act as a communications centre./

Conference material/ is a very important supportive tool./ Develop a central theme,/ a conference identity,/ much the same as a corporate identity,/ and use the layout/ or coloured paper/ for all communications,/ for example,/ name tags,/ registration cards,/ note paper,/ brochures,/ etc./ Delegates will need to be provided with/ presentation kits/ with all the relevant documentation:/ programmes,/ talk summaries,/ notepads,/ handouts/ and promotional items/ as giveaways./ Decide what the kits should contain/ and get these ready/ for distribution at the conference./

All practical arrangements,/ for example,/ the layout and seating at the venue,/ provision of equipment/and catering/ can be discussed with the venue staff./ As the conference date approaches/ a detailed run-through of the day/ is essential./ Make a checklist/ that you can refer to on the day/ to make sure/ that nothing has been overlooked,/ for example,/ flowers/ These can either create/ a wonderful atmosphere/ or make your conference venue/ look more like a funeral parlour!/

■ Task 8   Suggested answers

Budgeting plays a vital role. An effective budget is crucial to the success of the conference. Work out your costs. How much is needed for fixed costs, for example, the venue hire, speakers' fees and so on. Then calculate the amount needed for variable costs such as additional hotel accommodation, extra delegates' packs etc. Again, check your figures with the venue staff and ask for their input. And always allow a contingency of at least 10% to cover unforeseen expenses.

5 Complaints KEY

■ Task 1

A. 8
B. 5
C. 10
D. 9
E. 6
F. 2
G. 4
H. 7
I. 3

■ Task 2

1. C/E
2. F
3. A
4. B/F
5. D
6. D/E

■ Task 3

1. whinging
2. shedding their reserve
3. sussed
4. stand their ground
5. sparked
6. rash
7. timid
8. wary
9. stoical/keeping a stiff upper lip
10. fuelling
11. badmouth
12. doom and gloom

■ **Task 4**

A. 8
B. 3
C. 2
D. 9
E. 6
F. 1
G. 5
H. 4
I. 7

■ **Task 5**

Mr R Carey
Unit 7 Travis Industrial Estate
Bolton
BC2 5GE

14 July 20XX

Dear Mr Carey

Order No. TY 9642

We are writing with reference to the above order and our letter of June 28 in which we requested information about the delivery of the wallpaper. The original agreed delivery date of July 1st has passed and we have been trying to contact you by phone and email but have either not been able to get through to someone who knows about this order or there has been no reply.

Unless the wallpaper arrives within the next week, the completion of one of our jobs will be delayed and we will incur penalty charges. We would like to make it clear that we are holding you to your delivery contract, and that if we incur penalty charges because of late delivery, we will pass these charges on to you.

Yours sincerely

Mr B Askoy
Director

■ **Task 6**

1. for
2. of
3. to
4. on/by
5. for
6. in
7. to
8. in
9. with
10. of
11. of/in
12. off
13. out
14. of
15. to
16. to
17. beyond
18. to
19. with
20. in

■ **Task 7   Suggested answers**

1. Despite/In spite of
2. In comparison with
3. On the one hand ... but on the other hand
4. However
5. Although/Though/Even though
6. though
7. while/whereas/on the other hand/but/however

6 Proposals and reports KEY

■ Task 1 Suggested answer

The problem

As a result of Angela Weiss deciding not to return to work after her maternity leave, the Accounts Department has been left short-staffed. Consequently, some accounting and payroll functions have been suffering. Bringing in agency staff to cover these office activities results in considerably increased costs. Recruiting a permanent person will allow the department to function more effectively and reduce costs.

The goals

To ensure that the Accounts Department has an appropriate number of staff to meet the requirements of the Department.
The goals are:

▶ to provide professional accounting and payroll services
▶ to ensure that these services are provided at a lower cost than when they are dealt with by agency staff
▶ to guarantee on-time payroll and other account payables

The solution

Recruit an additional permanent staff member to the Accounts Department in order to allow this department to run in an efficient and cost-effective manner.

■ Task 2 Suggested answer

Local, regional & national activity points to the need for formal ITT/EPD training for teachers of Business Studies. No national strategy exists to provide them with rigorous professional learning or pedagogy. Training is ad hoc & reliant on collaborative networks which may be limited in sustainability. Funding will provide key teachers with time and resources to experiment & share best/innovative practice much more widely. Ours is not a passive outreach model: it is vital that others are empowered to lead e.g., in targets (mentor crossmoderation) 1.3 & 2.4 (peer training by primary mentors in year 4).

■ **Task 3   Suggested answer**

▶ Write full forms of abbreviations.
   ITT/EDP   ITT in an educational context stands for Initial Teacher Training.
   EPD   stands for Early Professional Development

▶ Avoid Latin/foreign language terms unless there is no alternative.
   ad hoc is a Latin term (to this) which means arranged or happening when necessary and not planned in advance.

▶ Explain concepts in terms a layman can understand.
   passive outreach model

Outreach means the activity of an organisation that provides a service or advice to people in the community, especially those who cannot or who are unlikely to come to an office, a hospital etc. for help.

"Passive outreach model" in this context means the college does not just want to use external bodies to supply the expertise they lack, they want to be active and learn about business for themselves.

■ **Task 4   Suggested answers**

1. The purpose/objective of this proposal is to ...
2. This report outlines the advantages and disadvantages/pros and cons of ...
3. Interestingly, ...
4. For the above-mentioned reasons ...

■ **Task 5**

2. ✓
5. maybe

■ **Task 6   Suggested answers**

On the basis of the findings above, it would seem that although the quality and retail prices of X products are competitive, a large percentage of consumers are not aware/unaware of the product range. Furthermore, many of those who are aware of the range do not find the packaging sufficiently attractive to induce them to purchase any of the products. Our recommendation, therefore, is that your company launch a new advertising campaign to increase consumer awareness, in addition to altering the packaging of the entire range so as to make the products more attractive/appealing to consumers.

■ **Task 7   Suggested answers**

1. C
2. F/D
3. D/E
4. A
5. B
6. E

■ **Task 8   Suggested answers**

▶ position in the organisation
▶ biases

■ **Task 9**

Primary information	Secondary information
questionnaires	pamphlets
experiments	journals
surveys	newsapers
observations	books
raw data (collected by yourself)	Internet
	reports
	magazines
	raw data (collected by others)

■ **Task 10   Suggested answer**

To: Head of Training, Gary Yim
From: Natascha Sowade, Assistant Training Officer
Date: 10th June 20XX
Subject: Staff Training 20XX

Purpose of the report

▶ To identify areas where training is needed
▶ To identify staff who would benefit from training
▶ To present available training courses
▶ To present the training budget for 20XX

Background

▶ Summarise staff training 20XX

Supporting data

▶ Areas where staff training is needed/has been requested
▶ Staff in need of/would like training
▶ Courses available: content, length, cost

Conclusions and recommendations

▶ Prioritise training needs as requests exceed the scope of the budget

7 Meetings KEY

■ Task 1

Own answers depending on your opinion

■ Task 2 Suggested answers

▶ Deviating from the main subject: ineffective chairperson, no agenda, unresolved conflict between participants

▶ Poor preparation: information not distributed beforehand, poor time management, too many handouts, full information not available

▶ Questionable effectiveness: no clear agenda, objective of meeting not made clear, lack of agreement on way forward

▶ Lack of listening: hidden agendas, ineffective chairperson, insufficient airtime

▶ Some participants talk too much: ineffective chairperson, lack of consideration for other participants, hidden agenda

▶ Length: time limit not given, time limit not adhered to, ineffective chairperson

▶ Lack of participation: lack of preparation, ineffective chairperson, fear of hierarchy, lack of motivation/engagement

■ Task 3   Suggested answer

AGENDA 23/03/20XX	New Developments
Location: Meeting Room 1/10am – 12pm	Participants: All Support Staff
TOPIC	TIME
Opening remarks	10.00 – 10.15
Proposed relocation	10.15 – 10.30
Departments affected	10.30 – 11.00
Coffee break	11.00 – 11.15
Discussion on way forward	11.15 – 11.45
Next steps and closing remarks	11.45 – 12.00

■ Task 4

1. consensus
2. midwife
3. intervening
4. scope
5. allotted
6. paraphrase
7. settle for

■ Task 5   Suggested answers

▶ back a particular opinion voiced in the group
▶ offer their own opinions
▶ let the group unconsciously shy away from a difficult area
▶ lead the group towards what they think is the right direction

■ Task 6

Expressions	Tasks
1. So, Alice agreed to ..., can we have your response by next week?	j
2. What do you think of ...?	g
3. Will a coffee break at 11 be OK?	d
4. I'd like to thank everyone for coming and ...	a
5. Can I just summarise the main points/views/problems?	j
6. Can we come to your point later, please?	h
7. May I suggest we begin by ...?	c
8. Great, could you outline the problem as you see it?	e
9. So, what you're saying is ...	f
10. OK, I suggest we finish. We've achieved our main objectives.	i
11. Can we all agree on this? Good, well let's move on ...	g
12. Now, as you probably know ...	b
13. Right, as we've agreed in principle to ... the only thing left is to ...	i
14. Mrs XYZ will take notes ... you'll all get a copy later	d
15. Just a minute Corinna, let Martina finish what she's saying	h
16. If I understand you correctly, you mean ...	f

■ **Task 7**

1. OK, I guess you're right ...
2. I think the move is a bad idea; I don't think so ...
3. Why don't we schedule them in?
4. No hang on a minute ...
5. Let me finish what I'm saying please ...

■ **Task 8   Suggested answer**

There's no doubt in my mind that it's a bad idea. People should be allowed to do what they want and we shouldn't be acting like the nanny state and commanding people what to do and what not to do. I think that if someone wants to smoke, they shouldn't be forced to go outside and, in any case, it means people will be spending a lot more time away from their desks. In my opinion, that'd be bad for the company. Therefore, I have to say that I totally disagree with the proposal.

■ **Task 9**

▶ Date, time, and venue of the meeting
▶ Participants present
▶ Opinions expressed
▶ Decisions made
▶ Next steps agreed, their deadlines, and the people responsible for them
▶ Date, time, and venue of next meeting

8 Writing promotional copy KEY

■ Task 1

1. c
2. a
3. f
4. e
5. d
6. b
7. g

■ Task 2

Can a mere radish drive customer loyalty? In a way, yes. We worked with a major grocer to develop a unique scale that identifies and prices produce through a plastic bag, so checkout queues move faster. Technology innovations like this, coupled with business innovations like RFID inventory control, give this grocer a real competitive edge. How did it happen? We put together a team of Supply Chain Management specialists, systems analysts and engineers who melded vendors, variable pricing strategies, and visionary (literally) scale. Want innovation for loyalty? Talk to the innovator's innovator: To learn more, visit:

■ Task 3

1. metaverse
2. blog
3. folksonomy
4. vlog
5. podcast

■ Task 4

1. We hope so
2. We'd beg to differ
3. we don't mean
4. All of which
5. it does

■ **Task 5**

logistical > logistic
teem > team
preps > props
places > place
reeled > rolled
Weather > Whether

■ **Task 6   Suggested answers**

1. Call 0800 325 7989 to order
2. Always lower/lowering prices
3. BUY ONE GET ONE FREE
4. Final days to save/get discount

■ **Task 7**

1. In addition > In addition,
   from > form

2. works > work
   it provides > they provide

3. to > too
   once > once,

4. slow > slowly
   let's > lets

5. grammer > grammar
   use > using

6. you look > you to look
   are > is

7. begining > beginning
   wont > won't

8. your > you're
   dictionnaries > dictionaries

9. neither > either
   which" > which"?

10. develope > develop
    carefull > careful

■ **Task 8   Suggested answer**

Group Overview

Vision

XXX's vision is to be a genuine leader in formulation science.

We have and will continue to build a portfolio of businesses that are major players within their respective industries, bringing together outstanding knowledge of customer needs with leading-edge technology platforms to provide superior products for our customers.

Through these attributes, we aim to create superior value for our customers and shareholders, without compromising our commitment to safety, health, and the environment and the communities in which we operate.

9 Apologising KEY

■ Task 1

1. b
2. a
3. c/b (in US English)
4. f
5. i
6. d
7. g
8. e
9. h

■ Task 2   Suggested answers

1. **I'm sorry**/Excuse me, I think we're supposed to be in this room.
2. This is proving difficult. **I'm sorry**/I regret I didn't book it earlier now.
3. **I'm sorry**, you can't take that book out of the library.
4. **I'm sorry**/I regret I won't be able to join you tonight. I've got visitors.
5. I'm sorry/I beg your pardon/Excuse me, what did you say?

■ Task 3   Suggested answers

1. Don't worry about it.
2. Well, let's get started, shall we?
3. That's OK

■ Task 4   Suggested answers

1. There are several methods, as outlined before, a company can use when looking to fill staff vacancies.

2. Headhunting is a costeffective way of hiring staff, and it works

3. Six applicants were short listed, out of 24.

4. Companies can justify the expense, and we know just how expensive it can be, of going to a headhunter.

Task 5

1. Only six people have replied to my memo?
2. It's true it's going to be difficult, but, there is a way we could ...

or,

2. It's true it's going to be difficult, but there is a way we could ...
3. I'm sorry, I wanted the figures for March, not February.
4. Wasn't it Jane who contacted Mr. Zappala before?

Task 6

1. The bank is writing a letter of apology to the letting agency because the bank failed to credit the agency's customers with the rent that had been paid. There was a delay in paying credits into the accounts of the addressee's clients.
2. Reimburse any landlord who has evidence that they have incurred bank charges, interest charges, or penalty charges as a direct result of the late payment of monies due.

Task 7

1. Let me once again apologise to you personally ...
   I am very sorry that ...
2. The fact is that you had properly instructed us to ...
   This delay was wholly caused as a result of our processing issue ...
   We were wholly at fault.
   ... our error ...
   ... it reflects a breakdown of the high standards that I have set locally.
3. ... and should not be taken as any reflection on your integrity and credit rating.
4. I can confirm that ... we will reimburse any ...
5. Hopefully ... will at least alleviate some of the potential consequences of our error.

■ Task 8

1. unfortunately
2. resulted in
3. remedy
4. made worse
5. beyond
6. subject to
7. in full
8. sincere

■ Task 9   Suggested answer

Our ref: MN 49OL85
Your ref:

Dear Ms Ramirez

With reference to your telephone call of 21st June, we would like to apologise for the delay in the delivery of your order for 6 X CJ 784510.

We have contacted the logistics company who have acknowledged the delay which, according to their Dispatch Manager, was the result of a fire at their depot. We can now assure you that delivery is scheduled for 4th July and we trust that this meets with your approval.

Once again, please accept our sincere apologies.

Yours sincerely

Pia Torreton

10 Giving presentations with impact KEY

■ Task 1   Suggested answers

Slide 1 – there's too much text which reduces impact; a boring font; no paragraphing

Slide 2 – the background image is irrelevant; the point size could be bigger; inappropriate action title

Slide 3 – it's unclear what the bars refer to; it's difficult to read the numbers; it lacks impact; there are mistakes on it e.g., 20010.

■ Task 2   Suggested answers

a) It has a poor title; confusing presentation; no source given

b) **Variations in Regional Poverty Rates**

Region	Percent Poverty
Region A	11%
Region B	22%
Region C	8%
Region D	43%

Source: 2006 Census

■ Task 3   Suggested answers

Don'ts:

▶ don't present a hard-to-read slide which only the people sitting at the front can read easily – make sure that the slides are legible and the whole audience can read what's on the slide regardless of where they're sitting

▶ don't fall into the trap of using pretty pictures – ensure the images are relevant – if it's just 'pretty,' it shouldn't be there

▶ don't use over-complex sentences – apply the KISS (Keep It Short and Simple) principle and avoid overly complex slides

▶ don't include distracting elements e.g., a huge logo on every slide or cartoons because they can detract from the message

▶ don't use lots of colours – keep them to a minimum to lend an air of continuity

■ Task 4   Suggested answers

1. Effect of high house prices on young people
2. Women still earn less than men
3. Secretaries have more responsibilities today

■ Task 5   Suggested answer

I HATE YOU

▶ you stole my boyfriend
▶ you were rude to my mother
▶ you frightened my dog

■ Task 6   Answers

1. Duration: *I plan to speak for about 10 minutes*

2. Introducing topic: *I'm responsible for organizing this Office Congress and I'd like to thank you for giving me the opportunity to talk to you about the two-day program.*

3. Questions: *and will be happy to take any questions at the end*

4. Outlining main points: *I'm going to divide my presentation into three main sections: the plenary sessions, the workshops, and the special lectures given by keynote speakers*

5. Introducing self: *First of all, I'd like to introduce myself. I'm from Company XYZ and my name's Helga Braun*

6. Greetings: *Good morning ladies and gentlemen*

■ Task 7   Suggested answers

a) Good morning ladies and gentlemen. First of all, for those who don't know me, I'd like to introduce myself. I'm Maria Schell and, as you may know, I'm responsible for organizing the program for our company in London. I am going to divide my presentation into three main sections, covering the events planned for Wednesday through Friday. I plan to speak for about ten minutes and I would be happy to take questions at any point if anything's not clear.

b)

Wednesday

6pm	Arrival at Heathrow + transfer to Marriott Hotel
8pm	Drinks in the hotel bar
9pm	Dinner in the hotel restaurant

Thursday

9am	Welcoming Speech by CEO
9.30am – 11.30am	Presentations SE Asia delegates
11.30am – 12pm	Coffee
12pm – 1pm	Round-table discussions
1pm – 2pm	Lunch in hotel restaurant
2pm – 4pm	Presentations German delegates
4pm – 4.30pm	Coffee
4.30pm – 5.30pm	Round-table discussions
7pm – 8.30pm	Urban Golf in Soho
9.30pm	Medieval Banquet at the Tower

Friday

9.30am – 11.30am	Meetings to agree on next steps
11.30am – 12.30pm	Closing speech by CEO
12.30pm – 2pm	Lunch at the Gay Hussars
2pm – 4pm	Sightseeing Tour of London
4pm – 4.30pm	Farewells
4.30pm	Departure to Heathrow

11 Team building and giving/receiving feedback KEY

■ Task 1

1. prone to
2. provocation
3. painstaking, conscientious
4. manipulative
5. offloads
6. averts
7. incidentals
8. discerning
9. dwells on

■ Task 2

1 *An* ideal team should have 2 *a* healthy balance of all 3 – nine team roles. 4 – Strong teams normally have 5 *a* coordinator, 6 *a* plant, 7 *a* monitor evaluator and one or more implementers, 8 – teamworkers, resource investigators or completer finishers. 9 *A* shaper should be 10 *an* alternative to 11 *a* coordinator rather than having both in the same team. In practice, 12 *the* ideal is rarely 13 *the* case and it can be helpful for 14 *a* team to know which of 15 *the* team roles are either overrepresented or underrepresented and to understand 16 – individuals' secondary roles. 17 – Team roles tend to develop and mature and may even change with 18 – experience and conscious attention. If 19 *a* role is absent from 20 *the* team, then it is often filled by someone who may not have recognized this role as 21 *a* dominant one. 22 *The* team should share their team roles to increase 23 – understanding and enable 24 – mutual expectations to be met.

■ Task 3

Carola is a coordinator and her allowable weakness is offloading work.

Emily is a teamworker and her allowable weakness is being indecisive.

■ Task 4   Suggested answer

Dear Carola,

I understand that you are under enormous work pressure, as we all are, but you did agree to arrange the location of the conference next month. You are the person with the most experience in this area and so I would be grateful if you could sort this out asap.

We are all working on this as a team and please rest assured that Emily will be taking responsibility for the equipment as usual. Thank you very much for your help and we are all looking forward to a very successful event.

■ Task 5   Suggested answer

Dear Emily

Further to your email correspondence with Carola, she will be responsible for deciding on the location. Further, we all agreed that you would be responsible for sorting out the equipment, so as soon as you hear from Carola where the conference will take place, could you get in touch with the centre and let them know what we need? We should all remember that we are part of the same team and have to pull together. Thank you very much for your help and we are all looking forward to a successful event.

■ Task 6

1. *OK I hear what you're saying; and anyhow, it's the first time something like this has happened so I don't think I need worry too much about it*
2. *in any case, what you said isn't quite true; the projector did actually work*
3. *but I had very little time to organize everything; I could have got things together much better*
4. *if you'd told me about the meeting a month in advance instead of a week*
5. *it's just that not all the participants could work it properly; it really isn't my fault if they got lost; I also really can't be held responsible for the weather*

■ Task 7

1. *Thanks for taking the time to talk to me*
2. *I know that things weren't perfect*
3. *what I'd really like to know is what suggestions you've got that would ensure that ...*
4. *it's always a learning curve for me to get feedback on an event*
5. *I'd like to know what I can do to make it better next time*

■ Task 8

It's unclear – what does "bugging" really mean? What exactly has happened "to drive them mad?" Who are "we?" There are also no constructive suggestions for improvement. It's impolite, disrespectful, and unprofessional.

■ Task 9

It presents factual information, uses "I," and invites a dialogue.

■ Task 10 Suggested answer

That report you wrote yesterday was really good. The introduction and summary were particularly clear and you kept to the point all the way through. It was very well-written and concise. Thank you.

■ Task 11 Suggested answer

To:	HR Dept.
From:	Anne X, PA to Bill Y CEO
Date:	31/08/20XX
Subject:	Courses on team-building and feedback

Mr Y has decided to run courses on the above as a matter of priority as the company is expanding fast.

Could you contact some external training consultants to find out:

▶ Length of courses offered
▶ Course contents
▶ Fees charged
▶ Client references

Please also draw up a list of possible participants.

I would be grateful if you could get back to me asap.

Anne X

12 Deadlines and reminders KEY

■ Task 1

1. worked out   entails   draft
2. standards   reckon
3. offload   completed
4. calling in   meet
5. slack   hitches

■ Task 2

1. up and running
2. teething troubles
3. hectic
4. draft
5. extent
6. break down into manageable chunks
7. milestone

■ Task 3   Suggested answers

1. Hi Jeanette, I was expecting to find the itinerary for Nicolas and Johanna on my desk this morning so that I could then finalise all the arrangements for their trip with them this morning. Have there been any problems?

2. Marc, you do know that the delegates' conference packs have to be got ready today, don't you?

3. Margot, I seem to be running low on headed paper. Shouldn't we have got our new stock of stationery by now?

4. Hi Paul, have you managed to draw up next year's holiday planner yet? I was hoping to have a look at it this afternoon.

■ Task 4   Suggested email

Dear Simon

I'm checking on what's happened to your draft of the advertisement. I haven't received anything from you yet and the deadline was yesterday. I have to have it ASAP because I need to go through it and then get it off to the magazine by close of work today in order for it to appear in next week's magazine. Please let me know if there are any problems so that they can be sorted out. Otherwise, please let me have the draft by 2pm today at the very latest.

Best wishes

Peter

■ Task 5   Suggested letter

Dear Mr Tricard

<u>Invoice No YT 7832</u>

Please let me first assure you that the above invoice has now been paid. Your bank statement should show $6,843.58 credited to your account Sept 15th.

I must apologize for the delay which was due to the introduction of new finance software. However, I am pleased to be able to inform you that the system is now fully up and running and we have ironed out any glitches. All future invoices will be paid on the due date.

I regret that you have been inconvenienced in this way but, hopefully, this will be the first and last time that it happens.

Yours sincerely

Jan Belmont

■ Task 6   Suggested second reminder

Dear Mr. Desai

I am writing concerning our order, No. PP 3528/c which we placed April 10th. The agreed delivery date was June 5th. The brochures had not arrived by June 8th and we sent you a reminder. The goods have still not arrived and we have received no explanation for the delay from you.

The brochures are needed for the trade fair in Hanover in July. If we do not receive the order in time, it will cause serious problems for us at the fair.

I would appreciate your immediate reply to this letter and a guarantee that the brochures will be with us by the end of June.

Yours sincerely

Nicky Tellekamp

■ Task 7   The correct conditional forms are in bold.

If this **sounds** familiar to you, you are almost certainly stressed out. Stress is constantly with us. What happens to you when you're under a lot of stress? Your heart races, your breathing gets faster, your blood circulation and metabolism speed up. Your muscles tense, getting you ready to fight or flee. But if you **don't** do either, it builds up.

Most people don't even realise they're stressed until they are about to reach boiling point. If something **had been** done about it earlier, unpleasant symptoms such as headaches, hypertension, insomnia, and abdominal pain could have been avoided..

80% of your worries never occur. If you **can do** something about it, do it. If you can't do anything about it, don't let it bother you. Stress can best be managed by realising what you can change about your life and knowing what you can't.

13 Saying "no" KEY

■ Task 1   Suggested answers

1. I'm afraid I'm not the best person to ask. I think Naomi's the one who deals with health and safety matters, isn't she? (You might phrase this as a question even when you know perfectly well that Naomi is in charge of fire notices.)

2. I'm sorry, I put my back out last week and I'm afraid it'll go again if I pick those boxes up. Shall I get Eve and Lee to move them?

3. I'm sorry, I'm up to my eyes in work today and don't have a minute to spare. Perhaps Bertil would look through them for you?

■ Task 2

a. 4
b. 2/4
c. 1
d. 5
e. 2/3/4

■ Task 3

1. E
2. B
3. D

■ Task 4

1. Thank you for putting aside some time
2. Before we go into that
3. If you'd let me finish/before we go into that
4. So, in order to avoid this happening, I've ...

■ Task 5   Suggested answer

Dear Johan

I would like us to find an hour this week so that I can express some concerns I have. I see from your calendar that we are both free on Wednesday 19th from 4pm to 5pm. Would that be convenient for you?

Regards
Sarah

■ Task 6

1. harasses
2. union
3. moral support
4. witness
5. offends
6. symptoms
7. grievance
8. tribunal

■ Task 7

1. point
2. find
3. nature
4. direct
5. such
6. constitute
7. making
8. directly
9. does
10. take

■ Task 8   Suggested answer

Dear Mr. Vozenko

I am writing to you to point out that I find one aspect of your behaviour towards me unacceptable, that is, the comments of a sexist nature which you make towards me. For example, at Monday's Department meeting you said, *Vanessa hasn't emailed me with the results of the survey yet, but what do you expect from a blonde?* This is by no means the only instance of such a remark.

I find comments like this unacceptable and I believe they constitute harassment in the work place. I am asking you to stop making such comments either directly to me or indirectly about me.

Should you continue to make sexist comments, I will have no alternative but to take the matter further.

Yours sincerely

■ Task 9   Suggested answer

Report of harassment

Department: ....

Date: ....

Time: ....

Details of person reporting harassment:

Name: ....

Position: ....

Name of line manager: ....

Details of person complained about:

Name: ....

Position: ....

Name of line manager (if different from above): ....

Nature of harassment e.g., racial, sexual, ...

Details of incident: Date: _____ Time: _____ Place: _____

What happened? ....

....

....

....

....

Who witnessed the incident? ....

14 Writing CVs with impact, covering letters, and letters of reference KEY

■ Task 1

1. e
2. g
3. c
4. d
5. a
6. f
7. b

■ Task 2   Suggested answers

Dos

▶ proofread it – no grammar or spelling mistakes
▶ ensure the CV looks professional
▶ make the headings clear
▶ include all the relevant points
▶ check for clarity and concision

■ Task 3   Suggested answers

Don'ts

▶ use jargon or slang
▶ use strange fonts or point size
▶ make it too long
▶ use clichés such as 'my profile', 'my career objective' etc.
▶ include trivia

■ Task 4

1. d)
2. a)
3. f)
4. c)
5. e)
6. b)

■ Task 5   Suggested answers

Dos

▶ lay it out professionally
▶ make it easy to read through using short paragraphs
▶ relate your skills/experience to the job ad
▶ include your contact details and date

Don'ts

▶ make it longer than one page – it shouldn't be an essay
▶ repeat what is in your CV
▶ ramble at length and stray from the point

■ Task 6

1. dog-eared
2. wishy-washy
3. bland
4. willingness to go the extra mile

■ Task 7

1. of
2. at/of
3. from
4. until/to
5. to
6. on
7. to/for
8. in/at
9. of
10. of
11. with/to
12. in
13. for
14. of
15. to

15 Conference invitations and requests for abstracts, cards for various occasions KEY

■ Task 1   Suggested answers

▶ Letter of invitation
▶ Conference programme

General information

▶ the venue
▶ travel
▶ catering arrangements
▶ accommodation – hotel booking form

Registration

▶ registration form
▶ special requirements
▶ contact details
▶ insurance
▶ Data Protection Act

■ Task 2

1. underway
2. contribute
3. cover
4. likely
5. presented
6. accompanied
7. including
8. submit
9. acknowledge
10. queries

■ Task 3

Dear ***,

1. I am writing to you in my capacity as Program Committee Co-Chair for the 18th Annual Computational Linguistics Conference, to be held in Hong Kong from October 1—8, 20XX. As you may know, the ACL conference is the premier

international conference of note in the field of computational linguistics and natural language processing. I am writing to ask whether you would be willing to present a talk at the conference as an invited speaker. Invited talks will be one hour long, including a 10 minute question & answer session.

2. We have not yet established on which day your talk would be scheduled; should you accept this invitation, there is some flexibility we can use to accommodate your own scheduling preferences (although it would be on one of the main conference session days, Tuesday October 3 through Friday October 6).

3. In appreciation of your agreement to provide an invited talk, ACL would provide the cost of an economy class airfare from your home institution to the conference, hotel accommodations during the conference, and free registration to the conference.

4. I will be away for an extended period and will not be able to read my email on a regular basis during this time. So please cc Professor Ida Grenville, an area chair and member of the ACL-20XX program committee, in your response. She has kindly agreed to coordinate the invited speaker sessions during my absence.

5. I do very much hope that you will be able to accept this invitation.

6. Yours sincerely

***

7. PS. If you accept our invitation to give an invited talk at the conference, you can choose to write a paper up to 8 pages long that will be included in the conference proceedings. Along with the paper hard copy, we request you provide a PDF file for inclusion in the CD-ROM version of the proceedings. If you choose to write a paper, please provide the hard copy and PDF file by August 1st. Please visit the conference webpage (http://www.cs.ust.hk/acl20XX) and click on "Instructions for Authors" for specific details on the formatting and submission of the camera-ready papers.

8. Regardless of whether you choose to provide a paper for the proceedings, we request you to provide us a title and an abstract (up to 200 words) by August 1st, 20XX.

■ **Task 4   Suggested answers**

A. 2, 4
B. 1, 3

■ **Task 5**

▶ Our sympathies for your loss.
▶ You and your family are in our prayers. ✓
▶ Martha will never be forgotten.
▶ Alex touched our lives and will be missed.
▶ You are in our thoughts and prayers. ✓
▶ You are in our hearts during this difficult time.
▶ Rachel's memory will live on forever.
▶ We are so sorry for your loss.
▶ James will live in our hearts forever.
▶ We share your sorrow.
▶ Thinking of you in these difficult times.

■ **Task 6**

1. on of
2. in of
3. to
4. in
5. to
6. in
7. to on
8. to to

■ **Task 7**

Congratulations on this great achievement. All the best.

How can someone who looks 40 have worked somewhere for 30 years? ✓

Wow! That's really something! ✓

20 years – you mad fool! ✓

Congratulations! And here's to the next 10.

Congrats! Do you get a medal? ✓

Congratulations on a memorable 15 years.

■ Task 8   Suggested answers

1. Just think, you'll be able to play golf every day if you feel like it!

2. Holidays in the sun, antique auctions, babysitting the grandchildren – ah well, you can't win 'em all!

3. No one deserves it more than you. You've dedicated so much of your life to all of us at Bexley's. Now it's time to put your feet up and relax!

4. Here's to days filled with fun and family.

■ Task 9

1. B,C
2. E
3. A/D
4. F
5. D
6. B,C

16 Influencing strategies and tactics KEY

■ **Task 1**

a. judiciously
b. getting someone on board
c. beware
d. threatening
e. intimidating
f. misleading
g. obnoxious
h. moans
i. sits on their hands
j. puts their heads above the parapet

■ **Task 2 Suggested answers**

1. Good evening, this is .... I am just calling to say that my room is very noisy. We've always been very happy with your service and have used your hotel on countless occasions so I'd really appreciate it if you could sort this out. I'm sure you'll be able to deal with this. Thank you.

2.

To:	Hans Brown
Subject:	Monday's presentation

Dear Mr Brown

I see from your email that you need some work done on your presentation for Monday. I don't know if you remember but you agreed last week that I could have a half-day off so I could go away this weekend. As you know, according to company policy, all employees are entitled to the occasional afternoon off if they arrange it with their superiors beforehand.

However, I do realise that your presentation is of high priority so what I suggest is that I will come in extra early on Monday morning and do the necessary work to it so that you will have it in time for your meeting.

I hope this solution is acceptable to you.

Best regards

3. "Hi Jenny, I just got your voicemail. I'm really sorry but it's the close of business here now so I won't be able to do anything tonight as I'm just on my way home. What I suggest is that you email the managers concerned today to save time. I'll follow it up with another email when we know when the meeting has been

rescheduled to. We're all part of the same team so I think it makes sense if we share the work. Hope this suits you and will be in touch tomorrow."

KEY TO MBTI TYPES

<table>
<tr><th colspan="3">Sensing Types</th></tr>
<tr><td rowspan="4" style="writing-mode: vertical-rl">Introverts</td><td>ISTJ</td><td>ISFJ</td></tr>
<tr><td>Quiet, serious, earn success by thoroughness and dependability. Practical, matter-of-fact, realistic, and responsible. Decide logically what should be done and work toward it steadily, regardless of distractions. Take pleasure in making everything orderly and organized – their work, their home, their life. Value traditions and loyalty:</td><td>Quiet, friendly, responsible, and conscientious. Committed and steady in meeting their obligations. Thorough, painstaking, and accurate. Loyal, considerate, notice and remember specifics about people who are important to them, concerned with how others feel. Strive to create an orderly and harmonious environment at work and at home.</td></tr>
<tr><td>ISTP</td><td>ISFP</td></tr>
<tr><td>Tolerant and flexible, quiet observers until a problem appears, then act quickly to find workable solutions. Analyze what makes things work and readily get through large amounts of data to isolate the core of practical problems. Interested in cause and effect, organize facts using logical principles, value efficiency:</td><td>Quiet, friendly, sensitive, and kind. Enjoy the present moment, what's going on around them. Like to have their own space and to work within their own time frame. Loyal and committed to their values and to people who are important to them. Dislike disagreements and conflicts, do not force their opinions or values on others.</td></tr>
</table>

Sensing Types	
ESTP	**ESFP**
Flexible and tolerant, they take a pragmatic approach focused on immediate results. Theories and conceptual explanations bore them – they want to act energetically to solve the problem. Focus on the here-and-now, spontaneous, enjoy each moment that they can be active with others. Enjoy material comforts and style. Learn best by doing.	Outgoing, friendly, and accepting. Exuberant lovers of life, people, and material comforts. Enjoy working with others to make things happen. Bring common sense and a realistic approach to their work, and make work fun. Flexible and spontaneous, adapt readily to new people and environments. Learn best by trying a new skill with other people.
ESTJ	**ESFJ**
Practical, realistic, matter-of-fact. Decisive, quickly move to implement decisions. Organize projects and people to get things done, focus on getting results in the most efficient way possible. Take care of routine details. Have a clear set of logical standards, systematically follow them and want other to also. Forceful in implementing their plans.	Warm-hearted, conscientious, and cooperative. Want harmony in their environment, work with determination to establish it. Like to work with others to complete tasks accurately and on time. Loyal, follow through even in small matters. Notice what others need in their day-by-day lives and try to provide it. Want to be appreciated for who they are and for what they contribute.

Extraverts

Intuitive Types	
INFJ	**INTJ**
Seek meaning and connection in ideas, relationships, and material possessions. Want to understand what motivates people and are insightful about others. Conscientious and committed to their firm values. Develop a clear vision about how best to serve the common good. Organized and decisive in implementing their vision.	Have original minds and great drive for implementing their ideas and achieving their goals. Quickly see patterns in external events and develop long-range explanatory perspectives. When committed, organize a job and carry it through. Skeptical and independent, have high standards of competence and performance – for themselves and others.
INFP	**INTP**
Idealistic, loyal to their values and to people who are important to them. Want an external life that is congruent with their values. Curious, quick to see possibilities, can be catalysts for implementing ideas. Seek to understand people and to help them fulfill their potential. Adaptable, flexible, and accepting unless a value is threatened.	Seek to develop logical explanations for everything that interests them. Theoretical and abstract, interested more in ideas than in social interaction. Quiet, contained, flexible, and adaptable. Have unusual ability to focus in depth to solve problems in their area of interest. Skeptical, sometimes critical, always analytical.

Introverts

Intuitive Types	
ENFP	**ENTP**
Warmly enthusiastic and imaginative. See life as full of possibilities. Make connections between events and information very quickly, and confidently proceed based on the patterns they see. Want a lot of affirmation from others, and readily give appreciation and support. Spontaneous and flexible, often rely on their ability to improvise and their verbal fluency.	Quick, ingenious, stimulating, alert, and outspoken. Resourceful in solving new and challenging problems. Adept at generating conceptual possibilities and then analyzing them strategically. Good at reading other people. Bored by routine, will seldom do the same thing the same way, apt to turn to one new interest after another.
ENFJ	**ENTJ**
Warm, empathetic, responsive, and responsible. Highly attuned to the emotions, needs, and motivations of others. Find potential in everyone, want to help others fulfill their potential. May act as catalysts for individual and group growth. Loyal, responsive to praise and criticism. Sociable, facilitate others in a group, and provide inspiring leadership.	Frank, decisive, assume leadership readily. Quickly see illogical and inefficient procedures and policies, develop and implement comprehensive systems to solve organizational problems. Enjoy long-term planning and goal setting. Usually well informed, well read, enjoy expanding their knowledge and passing it on to others. Forceful in presenting their ideas.

(Left margin label: Extraverts)

■ **Task 3   Suggested answers**

a. set up teams; create a good social environment; encourage them to participate actively in e.g., problem solving/brainstorming; use their natural presentation/ interactive skill; don't ask them to work alone on projects

b. don't expect them to participate a lot in meetings; give them tasks they can do on their own especially those requiring concentration; avoid interrupting them if possible; be a good listener

c. be specific and factual; outline plans in a logical fashion; provide fact-based support for your recommendations/suggestions

d. use their creative ability and original approach; don't overload them with detail; ask them to think out of the box

e. be well organized and to the point; support your recommendations/conclusions with data; be logical and objective; use their eye for detail to check analyses/ proposals

f. use their interpersonal skill for team building; ask them for their opinions on how decisions will impact people; be responsive to their highly developed interactive skills

g. be organised/efficient/structured; don't be late; don't make last-minute changes if at all possible

h. don't give them tight deadlines; be flexible and adaptable; be process-focused

17 Dealing with difficult people KEY

■ **Task 1**

1. balmy
2. drizzle
3. nuked
4. wriggling
5. dread
6. nippy
7. notch

■ **Task 2   Suggested answers**

hate; dislike; trying to make ... something it's not; miserable; freezing; nuked; wriggling with salmonella; covered in a thin film of ash; fills me with the same sort of horror and dread; flesh is starting to melt ... frozen solid; ridiculous; you won't be eaten by a mosquito; you won't die of food poisoning; you'll annoy ... a hot tin umbrella.

■ **Task 3**

The bulldozer

The bulldozer loves arguing and won't shut (1) *up* until they've had their say – so, let them run (2) *out of* steam. Obviously, if they are taking too much airtime, then butt (3) *in* any way you can and don't worry too much (4) *about* being overly polite. But whatever you do, don't argue (5) *with* them or disagree overtly (6) *with* them. Maintain eye contact and state your opinions assertively. Keep the floor and don't let them drown you (7) *out* as they often tend to have very loud voices – (8) *above* all, don't let things descend (9) *into* an undignified slanging match however tempted you might feel.

The sniper

The sniper can be downright mean and sarcastic yet often think they are being witty. This is the worst kind (10) *of* humour as it's always (11) *at* the expense (12) *of* someone else. Their favourite trick is to put others down (13) *in* public and they absolutely thrive (14) *on* taking a potshot (15) *at* every opportunity. To counter a sniper, you could paraphrase what they've said and ask them how and why their contribution is relevant (16) *to* the discussion (17) *at/in* hand as very often their comments are totally irrelevant and they're just doing what they're experts (18) *at* – sniping (19) *for* the sake (20) *of* it! If their comments are (21) *on/about* the matter

(22) in/*at* hand, don't go along (23) *with* their negative viewpoints – ask others what their opinions are and try to reach consensus. (24) *In* this way, you will take the wind 29 *out of* the sniper's sails.

■ Task 4

The loose cannon

(1) *The* loose cannon is very unpredictable, liable to explode for (2) – no good reason, and very embarrassing to be around – they thrive on throwing tantrums much like (3) *a* toddler who freaks out when they are forbidden to do something. Once they've gone ballistic, give them time to regain control of themselves but if this doesn't seem to be happening, then stop them any way you can – even if it means shouting "Stop!" You need to show them that you take their concerns seriously but, (4) – first and foremost, you need to bring (5) *the* temperature down for (6) *the* sake of (7) *the* whole group. If you can and you think it might help, have some one-on-one time with (8) *the* loose cannon and try to find out what sets them off.

The 'yes-to-everything'

The 'yes-to-everything' needs to be liked – they always try to please everyone and offend no one. So they say "yes" to anything and everything but have absolutely no intention of following through. Or they'll say "yes" to so many things that they'd have to work (9) – 24/7 to get everything done. One way of dealing with them is to let them know you value them and to listen carefully to what they say – there could be (10) – hidden messages beneath all that good humour. If you need them to fulfil (11) *a* task, give them very structured assignments with (12) *a* clear and doable deadline.

■ Task 5   Suggested answers

The 'silent-as-a-tomb'

A tactic you can use to deal with this type is to ask them open-ended questions, so that they don't have an opportunity to remain silent or produce monosyllabic replies. 'Silent-as-a-tomb' needs a lot of patience – wait calmly until they respond and don't even think about trying to fill those deadly silences with your own words, otherwise you'll be back to square one and they'll just revert to type and continue to contribute a big fat zero.

The out-and-out moaner

There are several ways of dealing with them: don't argue with them, listen to their complaint, and paraphrase the facts without hanging any negativity onto them. Don't agree with or apologise to them and try to move as quickly as you can to problem-solving mode. Point out to them that helpful and positive comments contribute far more constructively to group interactions.

■ **Task 6   Personal opinions**

■ **Task 7   Suggested answers**

1. This is how we do it
2. Have you thought about it from this angle?
3. It might work better if we ...
4. It's fine by me
5. I prefer Y
6. I'd like to say that ...
7. That's a good idea
8. We could cooperate
9. We need you on board
10. There are several ways of doing X

■ **Task 8   Suggested answers**

1. Non-assertive. This kind of response doesn't rock the boat, doesn't express what she really wants to say, and is unlikely to achieve the result she wants.

2. Aggressive. This kind of response is confrontational, unprofessional, and is likely to get Susanna fired.

3. Assertive. This response states exactly where Susanna stands in a clear and concise way, asks for a cooperative solution, and is more likely to get the result she wants.

■ **Task 9   Suggested answers**

1.

From: Sabine Greene
To: Gina Dervlin
Subject: Project ABC
Dear Gina As you know, we are supposed to be working jointly on this project however, whenever I have asked you to contribute, you have consistently said that you have too much work. Whilst I can sympathise with the position you're in, it's also making my life quite difficult. Could we meet to talk about this and come to some sort of solution together? Look forward to hearing from you. Best regards *Sabine*

2. Hi Angela, I got your voicemail. I'm sorry to hear you're so overloaded but unfortunately I'm in exactly the same position and I'd rather not take on anything

else right now. I'd really like to help you but just can't at the moment. I'm sorry and hope you can understand my position.

3.

From: Geraldine Shaw
To: Claire Taylor
Re: PowerPoint course

Hi Claire,

I got your message about the presentation. I understand the situation you're in but would like to make a couple of suggestions.

Firstly, we could get the graphics department to prepare the slides for your presentation this time – I have checked with them and they have the capacity.

Second, as you know, I booked and paid for the course two months ago and I'd really like to attend it because it'll help me prepare more professional presentations in the future which will definitely be of use to our department as we won't always have to rely on graphics to find the time at short notice.

I really hope we can agree on this and look forward to hearing from you.

Best regards

Geraldine

■ Task 10 Suggested answers

1. I regret that my report will be delayed.

2. Regrettably/I'm afraid I am unable to extend the deadline.

3. I'm afraid there might have been a misunderstanding. There is still EUR 5,000 outstanding on the account.

4. Could there possibly be a mistake in the information you sent us?

5. We would appreciate a fast response to our email.

6. I'm afraid I am unable to accept your kind invitation as I have a prior engagement.

7. I'm afraid there will a slight delay in getting the information to you.

8. Would you be kind enough to inform us when you have sent the brochure?

■ Task 11   Suggested answer

Dear Mr Oldman

We regret that we will have to move the date of our meeting from Tuesday August 2 to Thursday August 4. This late change in our appointment is due to the fact that our new CEO would like to take the opportunity to meet you too and he is only available on that day. Whilst we are fully aware that you had planned to go on holiday on Thursday, we would be very grateful if you could make alternative arrangements. We realise that will most likely cause you some inconvenience and are very grateful for your understanding. Thank you very much for your flexibility and we look forward to seeing you.

Yours sincerely

Francis Alerma